The
Government
Business Case Analysis

By Ron Klein

Belzon
The Definitive Source for Business Case Analysis
BCA

ISBN 1-933912-23-5

First Edition, January 2008

Westview Publishing Co., Inc.
P.O. Box 210183
Nashville, TN 37221
www.westviewpublishing.com

The *Government* Business Case Analysis (BCA)

Performing Structured Analyses in the Public Sector

By

Ron Klein

> Ron Klein and Belzon are
> known for their integrity,
> honesty, and business acumen.
> Time after time, they impressed
> their customers with their
> structured, methodical, and fact
> based analyses.
> - Colonel Tim Crosby

Dedication

It is unfortunate that disparaging comments about the government are so common in American culture. One of the unheralded but great boons of the accelerated globalization of the past decade is our ability to compare the progress of nations with respect to education levels, economic progress, personal freedoms, technology, the arts, health care and other measures of development. When one assesses progress or the lack thereof, invariably a major factor is the quality of the government. We know this from casual observation. If one walks from Laredo, Texas to Laredo, Mexico the contrast is stark. The people, the climate, and the soil are the same. The overwhelming reason there is better health care, education, and economic opportunities in one of these towns versus the other can be attributed to nothing other than government.

There are military and civilian personnel throughout the government who are conscientious, bright, capable, and dedicated to improving government operations. These individuals seek feedback, look at best practices wherever they can be found, and persevere against an organization resistant to change in order to improve the quality of services, reduce costs, improve operations, and, in the process, bring a well deserved pride to the workforce. In our work we have met hundreds of such government managers. Invariably they are driven by a self commitment to improvement. The first step in this journey is typically an honest assessment of where the organization is and what can be. It is to these capable and dedicated government managers that this book is dedicated.

Acknowledgements

Over the years of conducting Business Case Analyses, I have learned from many. I've seen excellent BCAs and ones that never should have passed even the most perfunctory of reviews. It is impossible to list the names of all who have contributed to our current understanding and execution of BCAs. Nevertheless, I would be remiss is I didn't acknowledge the other Belzon analysts who have taught me so much and contributed substantially to this guide. They are Tim Stone, Kristen Stennett, Greg Curtis, Carla Hinojosa, Calais Klein, Bo Bradshaw, and Chris Johnson. Without their constructive critiques, this book would not have been possible. Nevertheless, I remain responsible for any errors or obvious omissions.

About the Author

Ron Klein is the CEO of Belzon, a federal government services company that is oriented on improving the efficiency and effectiveness of complex government operations. He has over thirty years of direct experience with the government. He is a former economics professor. He has had a key role in several government studies ranging from small organizational issues to national industrial sector assessments. He has developed, conducted, and supervised Business Case Analysis (BCA) studies for a multitude of complex government operations. For further information the reader is referred to www.belzon.com/BCA. Ron Klein can be reached at rklein@belzon.com. Comments regarding this text are solicited.

Table of Contents

Preface   7
    Intended Audience 8
    How to Use This Book 8

Chapter 1. Introduction 9
    Executive Summary 9
    What is a BCA? 9
        BCA Types 10
    When is a BCA Appropriate? 11
        Using the Appropriate Tool 11
        Answering Broad Questions 12
        Self-Assessment Tool 13
    When Not to Conduct a BCA 13
        New or Unique Product or Service 13
        Single Criterion Decision 14
        Pre-Determined Conclusions 14

Chapter 2. Before You Begin 15
    Executive Summary 15
    Get Commitments Before Starting 15
    Resources Versus Expected Improvements 16
        Complexity of Questions 16
        Limitations 16
        Trade-offs 16
    Don't Expect a 100% Assured Answer 17
    Challenges to Anticipate 17
        Substantial Management Attention and Employee Time 18
        Policy Restrictions will be Quoted as a Reason to Remain with the Status Quo 18
        Sometimes the Facts Don't Matter 18
        Human Tendency for Selective Memory 18
        Emotions Affect Non-Cooperation or Outright Dissent 18
        Strong Orientation Towards a Piecemeal Approach Rather than a Comprehensive
        One 19
        Changes Threaten Established Relationships 19
        BCA Requires Significant Time From Best Manager......................19
        BCA is Contrary to Government Culture 19

Chapter 3. Getting Started 21
    Executive Summary 21
    BCA Approval Authority 21
        Single Manager 21

When multiple managers decide 22
Ad Hoc Council 23
Approval Authority Attendance at Key Decision Presentations 23
Key Decision Meetings 24
BCA Review Council 24
Selecting the BCA Research Team Members 25
Government or Contractor-Led Team 25
Out-Sourcing the Entire BCA 26
Using Integrated Product Teams (IPT) 27
Skills of BCA Analysts 27
Characteristics of Successful BCA Analysts 28
Changing Study Members During the BCA Process 29
Implementation Team 29
Government Contracting Personnel and the BCA 29
Table of Contents 30
The BCA Process 30
Phase 1 - Preliminary Research 31
Phase 2 - Primary Research 31
Phase 3 - Final Research and Documentation 31
Progress Reviews 32

Chapter 4: Commencing the Study 33
Executive Summary 33
Ensure Foundations are in Place 33
Initial Brainstorming Session 33
    Step 1 – List Traditional Difficulties 34
    Step 2 – Define the BCA Scope 34
    Step 3 – Identify Assumptions 35
    Step 4 – List Alternatives 36
    Step 5 – Identify Critical Features 37
    Step 6 – Identify Primary Risk Categories 37
    Step 7 – Determine Evaluation Methodology 38

Chapter 5: Preliminary Research Phase 40
Executive Summary 40
Preliminary Research Phase 40
Available Data and Comparison Measures 41
    Discovery Process 41

Proposed Modifications 41
New information 42
Alternatives 42
Internal Checklist..43
Preparing for the Project Definition Presentation 43
Provide a Read-ahead Summary 44

Recommended Presentation Sequence 44
Criticality of the Agreement on the Project Definition 47
Project Definition Documentation 47

Chapter 6: Primary Research Phase 49
Executive Summary 49
Introduction 49
Developing a Research Plan 50
Finalizing the Scorecard 51
Advantages of Using a Large Number of Scoring Factors 51
Disadvantages of Using a Large Number of Scoring Factors 52
Site Visits and Scoring 52
Operational Impacts..53
Risks 54
Risk Categories 54
Objectivity..57
Double-Counting 58
Scoring Risk 58
Keeping Risk in Context 59
Scoring Consequences 60
Risk Reporting Matrix 61
Weighting Risk Sub-categories 63
Cost Evaluations 63
Defining Cost 64
Single Purpose for Cost Evaluations 64
Multiple Purposes for Cost Evaluations 65
Cost Data Compatibility 66
Cost Sub-categories 67
Cost Assumptions..68
Forecasting Costs 68
Converting Findings to a Cost Scorecard 69
Sensitivity Analysis 71
Ancillary Findings 71
Emerging Results Presentation 72

Chapter 7: Final Research Phase 75
    Executive Summary 75
    Introduction 75
    Final Results Presentation 76
    Final Scoring 77
    Recommended Alternative 78
    Alternative Selection 79
    Documentation 79

Chapter 8: Implementation 81
    Executive Summary 81
    Completing the Study 81
    Implementation 81
    Summary 84

Appendix A: Helpful BCA Practices 87

Appendix B: Common Characteristics to Include in the Cost Section of DoD BCAs 89

Appendix C: Converting Cost Estimates to a Score 90
    Scenario 90
    Simple solution 90
    Develop a formula 91
    Example using the formula with a wider range 92
    Example with appropriate range 92

Appendix D: Other Reference Sources 95

Appendix E: Acronyms 96

Preface

Every undertaking involves opportunity costs; that is, every hour spent in one endeavor is time that is not available for a myriad of other tasks. Finance 101 courses teach Return on Investment (ROI) calculations, and public policy courses teach cost-benefit analyses. Scores of good finance texts exist, ranging from college textbooks to topics as specific as the analyses and assessment of derivatives, and at least one excellent text specifically addresses Business Case Analysis (BCA) in corporate applications.[1] So the question is, "Why write this book"?

The answer is twofold. First, after performing several BCAs for various federal agencies, Belzon analysts encountered a dearth of practical, hands-on guides to assist federal agencies in performing BCAs in the environment in which they operate. While texts tailored to corporate applications appropriately cover topics such as the value of extending one's brand and the tax consequences of decisions, such topics are not applicable to federal agencies. In addition, federal agencies encounter other difficulties, such as diffused authority and a lack of data—the absence of a comprehensive cost accounting system is just one example. Finally, large corporations are experienced in structured analyses and the BCA is often a relatively minor modification to existing tools and practices. Therefore, the first reason for this book is to provide step-by-step guidance for government analysts in structuring and performing BCAs, regardless of the government organization or the questions being asked.[2]

The second reason for writing this book is to advocate better governance of federal agencies. In our view, the two greatest impediments to improved government are indifference and a lack of understanding as to how to proceed. This indifference is born of many fathers, not the least of which is a lack of direction and knowing where to start. It is our hope that this book will provide substantive solutions to both impediments by providing step-by-step procedures for conducting a BCA. It is also our abiding desire to provide assistance to those who want to undertake an assessment of how their agency performs its mission, to identify the advantages and disadvantages of the alternative means of performing the mission, and to develop a realistic vision of what can be achieved, as well as the necessary resources to accomplish the transition.

---

[1] Schmidt, Marty. <u>The Business Case Guide</u>. 2nd ed. Solution Matrix Ltd: May 2002
[2] DoD has some good reference sources to aid in performing BCAs related to the acquisition of weapon systems and the lifetime logistics support of them. The <u>Performance Based Logistics: A Program Manager's Product Support Guide,</u> published by the Defense Acquisition University Press provides an excellent overview of why an orientation on high level performance metrics is preferable to detailed technical specifications. The <u>Department of the Navy (DoN) Guide for Developing Performance Based Logistics (PBL) Business Case Analyses</u> (November 2007) is a good BCA reference source. However, both of these guides focus more on *what* the BCA should include rather than *how* to perform the study.

Intended Audience

The intended audience for this book is government personnel who execute or review BCAs—especially those who have never been involved in the conduct of a BCA, have had only a peripheral role, or infrequently participate in the analysis and documentation of a BCA. In addition, this guide is written to be useful to senior managers who direct the BCA, as well as those who will be performing the research and analyses.

How to Use This Book

The senior manager who authorizes the study and ensures appropriate progress should read the entire book. Senior executives who approve studies and review assessments should read chapters one and two, although they may elect to skim the remainder of the text. Other readers may scan the entire book and only read those portions for which they have a primary role (e.g., risk or cost). In addition, this book can be kept as a desk-side reference for anyone involved in the BCA. For the most part, this book is organized sequentially so that the team lead can review the issues germane to the current phase of the BCA.

Chapter 1. Introduction

Executive Summary
The BCA is a structured tool that assists decision makers in collecting and assessing key information. Although each study is tailored to the operation being studied, the process itself is consistent. In some cases, a preliminary BCA may be conducted. The BCA is the preferred tool for making a decision when broad questions are asked and the decision is based on multiple considerations. In addition, the BCA is an effective self-assessment tool for an organization.

Some situations contraindicate a BCA. For example, new or unique products or services may not have enough information available for good decision making. Also, a decision based on a single criterion does not require a BCA. Further, the BCA should not be prepared to rationalize a pre-determined decision.

What is a BCA?
The BCA is a structured tool that assists decision makers in collecting and assessing key information. Not uncommonly, government personnel resist the notion of a *business* case analysis. After all, the government is not engaged in business operations. However, when government managers overlook this semantics issue, they see that many government operations do have parallels to commercial operations. A good BCA considers multiple decision factors, is fact based and unbiased, can be tailored, and compares alternatives in a consistent manner.

- Multiple Decision Factors
  Use a BCA when more than one factor should be considered in making a decision. For example, if a decision is based on cost alone, then a cost analysis rather than a BCA is the preferred analytical tool. A typical BCA considers between two and five major parameters in determining an optimal solution. Example parameters include response time, quality, cost, managerial effort, contractual workload, labor burden,[3] core competencies, risks, alignment of responsibility with authority, reduction or elimination of inefficient *stovepipe* organizational roles, retention of critical expertise, and so forth.

- Fact Based
  To be credible, the BCA must arrive at conclusions which are unbiased and supported by referenced facts. Removing bias is often a notable challenge in the conduct of BCAs. On one hand, personnel with ten or twenty years' experience have invaluable insight into what works and what doesn't. On the other hand, biases may exist for or against changes that are unsupported by current evidence. Although stories of failure often take on a life of their own, close examination often finds the error was an anomaly, was the result of a poor decision rather than a structural shortcoming, or has long since been corrected.

---

[3] For example, soldiers may have to perform additional maintenance actions such as cannibalizing parts from another vehicle to compensate for the lack of visibility into when the new spare will be received. While there may not be a direct dollar savings associated with the planned improvement, the advantages should certainly be clearly stated and considered in the evaluation of alternatives.

Providing empirical data or sources cited for each conclusion is imperative in producing an unbiased BCA.

- Tailored to Most Important Issues
  Study assumptions vary greatly; however, the BCA is a flexible tool and should be tailored, or structured, in a manner that provides fact-based analyses of the issues deemed important by the decision maker. In some instances the study scope is narrow and in other cases it is expansive. The number of alternatives considered may range from two to eight, and it may take between three months and two years to perform the study.

- Consistent Comparison of Alternatives
  The BCA evaluates alternatives, whatever the number. At a minimum, two alternatives are evaluated, typically the status quo and another option. In some instances, an industry best practice or unsolicited proposal prompts the manager to evaluate only two alternatives: to continue operations as they are or to convert to the proposed new method. Regardless of the number of alternatives, all should be evaluated, or *scored*, in a consistent manner. The variance in the availability of comparable data and/or similar past performance often makes this evaluation challenging; however, with the right BCA structure and discipline, consistent comparisons can, and should, be accomplished.

BCA Types

Each BCA is unique. Some have a limited scope and can be completed in as little as 90 days; others have an expansive scope with limited, available data and may take two years to complete. The relative importance of process quality, technology, capabilities, cost, and risk vary. However, despite the wide variance in BCAs, the process of performing the study is similar.

Although the content of each BCA is unique, the process is consistent.

In some cases conducting a preliminary or *feasibility* BCA is appropriate. Within DoD these studies are referred to as "Type 1" BCAs.[4] This type of study is appropriate to determine whether the perceived problem is serious enough to warrant the attention and resources of a BCA. For example, a known problem may exist with inventory management. If the magnitude of this problem is that the organization could occasionally improve economic order quantities and reduce back orders from 8% to 5%, then the optimal resolution may be improved practices that involve little management attention. However, if a feasibility BCA determines that the back order rate is

---

[4] In DoD, a comprehensive, or *formal,* BCA is referred to as a Type II.

10

22% and the best organizations handling comparable inventory are achieving a 3% rate, then a manager will likely elect to spend the resources to conduct a comprehensive BCA.

When is a BCA Appropriate?

We frequently hear people say that a BCA is just another name for process reengineering, quality improvement, or cost analyses. These comments reflect a lack of understanding of each of these process assessment and improvement tools. A brief summary of each of these tools follows:

- Process Reengineering

  Process reengineering (and process innovation) is structured processes used to determine the optimal means of performing an activity. These assessments typically benchmark a comparable best practice and then, whenever applicable, seek to reduce the number of steps in a process and/or incorporate overlapping steps in lieu of sequential ones.

- Quality Improvement

  Although a number of quality improvement tools exist, one of the most popular recent initiatives is the application of six sigma measures of variance. These improvement efforts typically endeavor to improve the quality of existing processes.

- Cost or Economic Analyses

  The government has extensive experience and approved models to project the costs of contemplated and/or funded projects. In many instances, the cost of one alternative is compared to the cost of another.

- BCA

  A BCA is a tool that is applicable when a manager wants to determine the alternative means to accomplish tasks and assess the relative scores of these alternative means against pre-determined multiple criteria (i.e., more than cost alone).

> None of these improvement methods is superior to another. The task at hand is to select the tool which is appropriate for the question being addressed.

Using the Appropriate Tool

It has been said that answers are easy; it is the questions which are difficult. If the question is how to improve an existing operation or service (e.g., reduce license processing time from 35 days to 15 days), then process reengineering is the applicable tool. If the question is how to improve the quality of services provided (e.g., accuracy of responses to IRS inquiries), then the manager should employ one of the quality improvement methods. If the manager has identified the alternative methods of providing a product or service and wants to make a decision based on the respective cost of each, then a cost analysis is the choice.

Answering Broad Questions

BCAs should generally be reserved for broader questions. For example, a manager may ask, "What is the optimal means for us to repair and return aircraft propellers? Should we perform these repairs in government facilities? Should the repairs and returns be outsourced to another government agency? Should they be outsourced to a commercial firm? What are the best practices, commercial and government, that we might be able to adopt?" The decision as to the optimal solution should consider the risk of not having repaired propellers available when they are needed, the cost of each alternative, the impacts to the U.S. industrial base, and the retention of critical government skills.

A BCA is an ideal assessment and management information tool when a decision is based on multiple considerations.

In the previous example, a government manager has decided that the decision as to how to *best* overhaul and repair propellers should be based on four criteria: improved repair and return process, impacts to the U.S. industrial base and U.S. government, risk considerations, and cost. In addition, the relative importance of each criterion is identified. In this instance, the BCA evaluation criteria might be something like this:

Evaluation Criteria	Individual Weight	Total Weight
Improved repair and return process		40%
Improved quality of repairs	30% *(12% overall)*	
Faster turnaround time of repairs	50% *(20% overall)*	
Process improvements applicable to other components	20% *(8% overall)*	
U.S. industrial base and U.S. government capabilities		10%
Risk considerations		15%
Cost		35%

Chapter 3 describes the process of determining evaluation criteria.

Self-Assessment Tool

A BCA is also effectively used as an organization's self-assessment tool. For example, a newly assigned manager may question whether the processes in place have evolved over time and remain in place because of comfort, knowledge, or a lack of knowledge of comparable best practices. In this instance, a manager may request a BCA in the first 180 days of the assignment. The BCA is not required but, rather, performed in order to document existing practices, identify what performance improvements are available, and which areas of the operation will bring the greatest gains.

A BCA can be an effective response to the "We've always done it this way" sort of thinking.

When <u>Not</u> to Conduct a BCA

When a new business idea is incorporated, a tendency for the language and tool to become trendy exists. When this happens, managers often begin using popular new methods to show that they are well-read and adept at embracing improvements. Therefore, it is important to also recognize when a BCA is *not* the right tool.

New or Unique Product or Service

The commencement of a BCA presumes the decision maker has a general idea of alternative performance methods for a particular function. Sometimes, however, the product or service is so unique and/or new that it isn't clear what process or processes should be used. In this case, a preliminary investigation should take place before forming a BCA team and assigning deadlines and allocating resources.

If alternatives are not known, it is premature to conduct a BCA.

Single Criterion Decision

Do not perform a BCA if the pending issue can be resolved by a single decision criterion. Other methods are more effective for single issue topics (such as customer wait time, cost, or quality improvements).

Pre-Determined Conclusions

A BCA should not be conducted if the preferred outcome is already known. For example, Belzon analysts were asked to assist with a BCA to determine the optimal means to provide aircrew and maintenance training for a new Army helicopter. In one of the preliminary meetings, an experienced BCA leader asked, "Does anyone in this room believe that our research and analysis may result in military aviators being trained at any place other than the Army's aviation school?" No one thought this was feasible. In this instance, a two-page memorandum documented the rationale related to why it is appropriate that the Army retains direct responsibility for all combat aviation training at their single, established school. This completed the action and no further analyses or documentation was ever requested.

The BCA should not be prepared to rationalize a pre-determined decision.

Chapter 2. Before You Begin

Executive Summary

The BCA study may require from three months to two years, depending on the complexity of the operation and the number of unknowns. Like all management decisions, the resources allocated to the conduct of a BCA should be commensurate with the projected improvements. The senior manager needs to make a decision as to when greater fidelity of information (higher confidence in the empirical data underlying the conclusions) is worth the corresponding higher cost and longer timeline.

The conduct of a BCA is often a substantial undertaking and should not commence without the requisite senior management *participation* in place. BCAs require analyses and self-criticism that is often difficult. The sponsoring manager is served well by understanding the resources required and the challenges associated with performing these analyses.

Get Commitments Before Starting

The conduct and documentation of a good BCA is a difficult endeavor. Do not initiate a BCA without first achieving the following decisions and commitments.

- Identify the Primary Sponsor
  Who is the primary manager with the interest in these analyses and the responsibility for the current process? Who is providing the resources? Who will identify the key aspects of the study? The primary manager needs to be involved and have the necessary clout to open doors and overcome resistance. If this individual is an unwilling or only slightly enthusiastic sponsor (e.g., the BCA is someone else's idea or requirement), the likelihood for success is severely lessened.

- Identify the Senior Level Participation
  Sometimes this is an existing board or senior group, or it may be a group assembled for this particular BCA. Frequently this is the next higher manager of the primary sponsor. The BCA is much more likely to succeed if this individual actively participates, and all those with whom the BCA team works with know of this senior leader's active participation (not just interest).

- Identify the Tentative Timeline and Key Milestones
  The overall time available for the study should be identified, as well as the general time allocated for each of the three phases. (See chapter 3 for more information.)

- Come Mentally Prepared
  Know that the process will get bogged down. Personnel who have information that is needed, will be busy elsewhere. Data will either not be compatible or not available. It will take discipline to avoid procrastination when it gets hard. Plan on it.

Resources Versus Expected Improvements

This guidebook applies to a wide range of government BCAs; therefore, it is impossible to provide specific answers to the questions of how much time and how many personnel to allocate to a BCA. More importantly, this is *and should be* the prerogative of the primary manager.

As with any undertaking, consider the resources required in comparison to the improvements expected. For example, one performance metric used by U.S. auto insurance companies is the time elapsed from a policy owner's accident until a settlement check is received. One insurance company measures this in weeks and another in minutes. If the process being evaluated is considering this sort of magnitude of change, it is likely that the analyses will require some in-depth research to ensure the risk is known, and to provide the requisite supporting documentation to embark on such a radical redesign. Sometimes this principle is understood more easily in reference to funds. For example, if contemplating alternatives which have the potential to save the government $50,000, a manager normally wouldn't elect to spend $40,000 determining the optimal solution. Conversely, if the projected cost savings are in the range of $12 million, then $500,000 and nine months for a thorough BCA may be necessary and appropriate.

Don't spend more on the analysis than the resulting answer is worth.

Complexity of Questions

Another consideration is the complexity of the questions being asked. For example, in one case the government had a long established support procedure in place for a relatively straight-forward product. A proposal was received stating that a commercial firm could perform the activity with better results and at a lower cost. Since the scope was limited, there were few unknowns, and data were readily available, two analysts completed this BCA in three months. However, in another instance, the services required were ill-defined, the products and services were large and varied, and comparable data were difficult to determine and document. This BCA was completed by five analysts over the course of nine months.

Limitations

Oftentimes a BCA must be completed by a certain deadline. This may be a contract renewal decision or, in DoD acquisition, a milestone decision. In these instances, the manager may have little latitude with respect to the time available for the BCA process and may consequently be limited to decisions regarding the scope of the BCA and the number of analysts participating in the study.

Trade-offs

A trade-off between greater fidelity of information and the cost of collecting, analyzing, and documenting the analysis always exists. If the projected outcome is to substantially alter an organization's roles or affect personnel, the results will be controversial and likely to require a more thorough analysis. On the other hand, if the purpose of the BCA is to provide a manager with information on which to act, without appreciably impacting other agencies or requiring approval from higher headquarters, then the depth of analysis may be less.

More in-depth and accurate information costs more time, money, and personnel. It is the responsibility of the respective manager to choose the right trade-off.

Don't Expect a 100% Assured Answer

A BCA typically will not result in a 100% assured best solution for three reasons:

1. Rarely is it appropriate to expend the resources necessary to achieve a 95%-assured solution. More empirical data can be gleaned and documented, more examples provided to increase one's confidence in the data, and a more thorough understanding of the facets of each alternative can always be achieved; however, more research requires more resources. If it takes three analysts six months to develop an 80% accurate solution, it may well take six analysts two years to develop an answer with a 95% *confidence coefficient*.
2. As the world continues to change, organizations and missions change, and technology and best practices evolve. Therefore, the longer it takes to complete a BCA, the more likely it is that an external change may alter the assumptions and invalidate much of the analysis.
3. A good BCA is a valuable component of the factors needed to make the best decisions, but it is only *one* of the factors that management uses to make a decision. Frequently, political, policy, and other factors must also be considered.

Challenges to Anticipate

Conducting a BCA is a challenging endeavor. The BCA inevitably requires extensive time from key personnel in gathering information that only they have. One of the primary lessons learned from the past fifteen years of process reengineering and process innovation is that collecting information is very disruptive to organizations. When the change process is abandoned before completion, the result is havoc to employee morale and the institution, and wasted funds. Although dramatic organizational change is sometimes necessary for a company's survival in a competitive marketplace, this imperative is rarely the case for government organizations. A manager should not casually embark on a BCA.

Conducting a BCA is government at its best. That is, it reflects an earnest desire to better perform the organization's mission(s). Whether it is a service to a taxpayer, a soldier, or businesses, the pursuit of improvement in how government functions is one of the most laudable endeavors in this nation, but be prepared to encounter many obstacles. The following partial list of challenges should dissuade the less-than-committed manager from embarking on this path.

Substantial Management Attention and Employee Time

Regardless of whether the manager elects to use personnel on staff or to hire an outside contractor to perform the analysis, the BCA process diverts attention from the organization's primary mission. For example, only current employees know the steps, written and unwritten, of current processes and required interview time detracts from the time they give to their assigned duties. Many of the Subject Matter Experts (SMEs) for specific processes have additional significant responsibilities. Participation in a BCA project or an IPT is typically viewed as an additional duty. The level and quality of the participation will be reflective of the management emphasis and the individual perception of the overarching motives. Decisions as to the appropriate scope, risks, critical success factors, and BCA scoring can only be made by the sponsoring manager. While a BCA can be structured to mitigate this impact, some of it is inherent in the process.

Policy Restrictions will be Quoted as a Reason to Remain with the Status Quo

Although the end objective is to improve government operations, one frequently encounters blind compliance to actual or perceived policy or regulations that ostensibly prohibit changes. Even if the policy applies to the alternative being considered, analysts should bring this to the attention of the decision maker. Justifying and requesting an exception to policy should be the prerogative of the study sponsor.

Sometimes the Facts Don't Matter

This is particularly true when changes will potentially result in the elimination or relocation of jobs or promotion potential. Sometimes there are especially strong political influences which override planned efficiency improvements. An astute manager knows which battles can be won and doesn't unnecessarily expend resources and credibility on those which will be lost.

Human Tendency for Selective Memory

We generally remember our successes and the failures of others, while transposing those memories based on our perception of others. This type of halo effect can apply to individuals or entire organizations. Organizational memory can be lacking for causation and adjustment, and can lead to a lack of empirical data or the appearance of quality data which is not entirely accurate. For example, an organization can be tasked with a certain level of performance and if it becomes obvious there will be a shortfall, the goals or objectives may be adjusted to demonstrate success.

Emotions Affect Non-Cooperation or Outright Dissent

Considering changes to current practices, particularly those performed by existing government employees, is fraught with pitfalls. Proactively addressing spoken and unspoken, and often unrecognized, concerns requires strong managers. For example, once analysts begin to document the efficiency of an operation, a risk of discovery exists that current employees might not be as knowledgeable or as productive as believed. The types of questions asked may cause anxiety if the source begins to suspect that another process should be implemented, thus diminishing the perceived value of the employee or the organization. Furthermore, if the findings are that the process should be outsourced, then the inference may be that current employees are incapable or unmotivated. Inquiries into how the government process functions in comparison to best commercial practices may highlight how little someone knows about comparable industry trends.

Strong Orientation Towards a Piecemeal Approach Rather than a Comprehensive One

Part of the reason for the piecemeal approach is the organizational structure, and part of it is due to pride in the aspect of the job that one knows. The result is that when an analyst begins to define status quo, it becomes obvious that many actions operate exclusively of one another. Often no single person understands the entire process flow. The simple act of requesting this status quo information can cause skepticism and hesitancy, and the lack of understanding of the entire process can cause friction and have a significant impact on the quality of the information given.

Changes Threaten Established Relationships

Humans are relationship oriented. We establish relationships with other employees, vendors, and contractors. In all but the instances of egregious relationships, we resist altering these established and comfortable relationships.

BCA Requires Significant Time From Best Manager

The conduct of a BCA requires an especially strong manager who is open to new ideas and is experienced in affecting organizational change. Although effective managers are generally good delegators, delegation needs to be limited on the BCA. If subordinates begin making decisions regarding which alternatives are viable, which policies will dominate decision, or what research and documentation is not required, then the validity of the BCA is jeopardized. To ensure the manager does not need to delegate authority, structure the BCA in such a manner that the manager's time and attention with the BCA process are deliberately limited (for example, use capable and experienced outside consultants on the BCA team). Despite the natural reluctance to assign the best managers to assist with a BCA, their participation is imperative to the success of the study.

BCA is Contrary to Government Culture

Every organization has a culture and values. Organizations are constructed and redesigned to achieve particular outcomes. Consequently every organization encounters endeavors that are difficult for them. In many respects, the BCA process is one of these.

A minority of the improvements sought by industry succeeds and companies have the imperative of survival in a competitive environment. Pursuing and, more importantly, implementing such improvements in the government is much more challenging. Do not embark on this course without understanding its difficulties and having the resolve and the commitment of senior leadership participation.

Chapter 3. Getting Started

Executive Summary
An often overlooked but crucial step in the setup of the BCA is the identification of the authority who will review, modify, and/or approve the study findings and recommendations.

The BCA team members may be government personnel or contractors. There are advantages and disadvantages to each arrangement. Including experienced BCA personnel on the team is helpful with respect to understanding the structured process, reducing common process errors, and having a knowledge of comparable best practices. While specific skills are valuable in the selection of study analysts, having appropriate research abilities and attitudes are also important. It is especially disruptive to have turmoil on the BCA team once it is established.

A three-phased approach is recommended for the conduct of BCAs. These three phases should be distinct; that is, a subsequent phase should not begin before the earlier phase is approved. Three formal presentations are strongly recommended: the *project definition*, *emerging results*, and *final results*. All who will have noteworthy impact as to whether the study recommendations should be implemented should be present or represented at these three key decision points.

BCA Approval Authority
Identifying the authority who will review, modify, and/or approve the study findings and recommendations is a crucial step in the setup of the BCA. Sometimes the reviewing authority is an individual and at other times it is a board or council (established or ad hoc). The reviewing authority's sole purpose is to provide senior leadership participation in the BCA.

> Work on the BCA should not commence before everyone is clear as to who will review and approve the study results.

Single Manager
If the operation being assessed is within the purview of a single manager, then the manager may elect to be the sole person who charters the BCA, approves the study parameters, and accepts the findings and recommendations. In some cases, the manager who requested the BCA has the responsibility and authority to implement the recommendations. If this is the circumstance, then BCA analysts have an easier staffing and coordination task. In this situation, the approval process is straightforward and this manager approves the study parameters (e.g., scope, assumptions, alternatives, evaluation methodology), receives interim progress updates, approves or alters the emerging findings, and decides which aspects of the final recommendations to implement.

When multiple managers decide

Major improvements frequently come from process redesign or improvement initiatives that take an enterprise approach to the task, rather than a segmented one. The scope of the BCA will be to compare alternative means to achieve end objectives. That is, to look at the *entire* process. A BCA with a comprehensive scope invariably overlaps organizations. When this occurs, the BCA findings and recommendations will be reviewed and decided by multiple managers.

For example, within the DoD, different organizations are responsible for the maintenance and support of an aircraft engine. One agency has responsibility to purchase the engines, another has the overhaul, another has the training of maintenance personnel, another has the transportation of engines being returned for maintenance, and another one for spares management. A consequence is that each agency can optimize their aspect of engine sustainment, but at the expense of another. (For example, a transportation specialist can excel at bundling shipments to reduce transportation costs, but is unaware of the impact on overhaul maintenance manpower scheduling or the need to procure new engines to compensate for shortages.)

Major improvements frequently come from process redesign or improvement initiatives that take an enterprise approach to the task rather than a segmented one.

Any time other organizations may be affected by the implementation of the BCA recommendations, managers for these groups should participate in the study's key decisions. Although participation does not imply that the concurrence of these (potentially) affected managers is necessary, it may be entirely appropriate during the *staffing* action for an affected manager to express non-concurrence and provide supporting rationale. This consideration of the facts and input of affected managers is the role and responsibility of the *senior deciding executive*. While there are several reasons to have affected managers participate in the BCA, a primary one is to ensure the study is comprehensive. If the BCA analysts have faulty explanations of the current process or effects of the recommendations on other organizations, the credibility of the BCA will be suspect.

In one instance, an organization that would have been adversely affected by changes in program funding was only consulted during the final review. The projected funding shortfall for the other agency couldn't be satisfactorily resolved and, consequently, the final recommendations were not approved. Whether the outcome of this study would have been different if this issue had been raised and considered early in the analysis will never be known. What is certain is that substantial resources were expended on the study which was performed under the assumption that this funding issue would not be a deciding factor.

Any time other organizations have the potential to be adversely affected by the study recommendations, these managers should participate in the key BCA decisions.

Ad Hoc Council

In some instances, the manager may choose to form an ad hoc board of other senior executives in order to solicit the perspective of experienced managers who have some distance from the operation being evaluated. Such an advisory council can provide valuable external views, although their input may be advisory only and not have any authority related to the final decision. Such delineations should be made in writing (e.g., whether members will vote, have veto authority, or have solely an advisory role).

Forming an ad hoc advisory council is advisable when multiple organizations may be affected by the redesign process being considered. This council should include senior leaders of the affected organizations and, in some cases, specialists. This council (or *board*) provides four crucial advantages to the BCA:

1. By participating in the project definition and reviewing the findings, the council helps ensure that the right questions are being asked.
2. Members of the council often assist in data gathering if the BCA analysts encounter difficulties.
3. The council generally participates in the analytical process and assists in the approval of recommendations for which they are responsible.
4. Personnel and organizations are naturally reluctant to find fault with themselves. An external review board frequently helps delve into appropriate areas and document its findings.

Approval Authority Attendance at Key Decision Presentations

BCA analysts must ensure that the approving manager is present for key study decisions. It is not uncommon for managers to have scheduling conflicts and, therefore, delegate meetings and decisions to subordinates. While this can, and should, occur with routine matters, the presence of the final approving manager at the project definition presentation, the emerging results presentation, and the final results presentation is essential—even if it is means rescheduling others' appointments.

The presence of the final approving manager at the project definition presentation, the emerging results presentation, and the final results presentation is essential.

If the operation being evaluated crosses the boundaries of other offices or agencies not under the control of the study sponsor, senior members of the affected organizations also should attend key decision presentations, specifically, the three primary milestone presentations: project definition, emerging results, and final results. It is absolutely necessary that anyone who will eventually review the final report and have influence over accepting the findings related to implementation will be present or represented at these key decision meetings.

 All personnel with influence over the final report should attend the three primary milestone presentations: project definition, emerging results, and final results.

Key Decision Meetings

The *project definition* meeting defines the scope of the study, establishes assumptions, identifies alternatives, and determines the evaluation methodology (sometimes referred to as the scoring method). Most major disagreements related to BCAs are traced directly back to the underlying study assumptions and methodology. Senior managers with authority over operations that may be affected by changes to an operation, and those with relevant experience, may well have differences of opinion as to what should be included in either the study or the deciding factors. These issues need to be identified, addressed and resolved before phase 2 commences.

The purpose of the *emerging results* presentation is to learn of any additional research that is needed and to provide the decision maker(s) with notice of potentially controversial findings.

The *final results* presentation is comprehensive, but does not include substantial surprises. Recommendations include general milestones and activities, but not detailed implementation planning.

BCA Review Council

If multiple BCAs are performed or planned within an organization, the senior organization should establish a BCA *review council*. This group should meet not only to provide final approval, but also to assist in the entire BCA process. The higher headquarters should establish procedures for the conduct of these studies. For example, the headquarters should provide a checklist for the questions that need to be answered prior to approval to commence a BCA, another checklist of the issues that will be addressed at the *project definition* presentation, and a third checklist identifying the questions that will be asked at the *final results* presentation. These checklists will ensure consistency, and aid those preparing BCAs by providing specific guidance rather than seemingly arbitrary disapprovals, or re-work that is required after the study is complete.

Selecting the BCA Research Team Members

The selection of the BCA analysts largely determines whether the study is completed on schedule and is comprehensive, unbiased, and credible. The following team selection considerations are offered.

Government or Contractor-Led Team

Although teams can be comprised of government employees, contractors, or both, experience indicates that mixed teams typically do not work very well. Government personnel cannot (and should not) be supervised by contractors, so the result of a mixed team is that the BCA-experienced analysts are unable to lead the study effort. Consequently, either inexperienced analysts supervise experienced personnel, or leadership is diffused with no one being responsible for progress.

 The conduct of a BCA has a learning curve. Using experienced BCA personnel lessens errors, includes knowledge of applicable best practices elsewhere, and increases the likelihood that the BCA will be completed on time.

Sometimes, however, a mixed-team arrangement may be necessary and, even, advantageous. For example, if the government office anticipates conducting multiple studies over the upcoming years, it can use this arrangement to learn how to structure and perform BCAs. Also, the availability of resources often affects the BCA team structure. For example, if a manager does not have the financial resources to hire a contractor team, then the decision to use a government team is a forgone conclusion. Conversely, if the all the capable government personnel are fully engaged and the manager has funding for such a finite project, a team of contractor BCA personnel is likely the obvious choice. Tables 1 and 2 list the advantages and disadvantages of using government or contractor BCA analysts. The advantages and disadvantages of a contractor BCA team are the opposite of those of a government team.

Table 1. Advantages and Disadvantages of Using Government BCA Analysts

Advantages
• Personnel are thoroughly familiar with both the *as-is* model (current operation) and the requirements.
Disadvantages
• Generally this assignment adds an additional duty to a person's normal responsibilities, constraining the time and attention that the analyst can dedicate to the BCA.
• The conduct of a BCA is a skilled process in itself, and unless the government analyst has performed BCA analyses before, missteps and errors are likely to occur.
• Generally speaking, government personnel are not familiar with best industry practices or comparable government process. They have not attended commercial oriented symposiums and conferences and are likely to be unfamiliar with recent developments in commercial practices or to know which ones may be applicable to the government operation.

Table 2. Advantages and Disadvantages of Using Contractor BCA Analysts

Advantages
• Experienced contractor BCA-analysts are knowledgeable in all aspects of conducting a BCA, ranging from group dynamics, research sources, corollary commercial practices, appropriate depth of data collection, time requirements for report editing and the preparation of presentations.
• Generally speaking, contractors have less latitude to slip delivery dates and frequently push through inevitable blockages.
• A contractor BCA-analyst team is typically dedicated solely to this BCA for the contracted time, resulting in fewer *high priority* actions that divert it from the study.

Disadvantages
• Typically, the team is not familiar with the current operation or the myriad facets of end customer requirements which are undocumented.

After considering the advantages and disadvantages of both types of teams, if the decision is made to rely on a contractor-led BCA team, the government must identify a *primary coordinator* who is thoroughly familiar with the government operation being analyzed. The primary coordinator provides three primary functions:

1. Explains to the analysts how the current operation works, what the traditional difficulties have been, and what aspects of performance are important to the end user.
2. Acts as a liaison between contractors and government personnel, when they are unresponsive or reluctant to provide information to contractors.
3. Provides information to the study sponsor and other government personnel and reduces the amount of time the analysts need to explain their actions and progress.

The caliber of government personnel and/or the primary coordinator directly affects the timeliness, and thoroughness, credibility of the final BCA.

Out-Sourcing the Entire BCA

In some instances the entire BCA research process is outsourced to either a contractor or to an experienced government group. The rationale most often given for this approach is that existing government personnel have neither the time nor the expertise to conduct the analysis. This approach has a moderate risk for failure because the outside team does not have knowledge of the operation being assessed or awareness of the unwritten lessons learned. The sponsoring government manager often feels less engaged and, hence, is not as available to assist with the inevitable logjams. Most significantly, those who have the implementation responsibility have too little ownership. Far too often, these BCAs meet an external requirement and then become one more costly study sitting on a shelf collecting dust.

However, when the outsourcing approach is taken, steps can be taken to mitigate the risk that the final analyses and recommendations will be ignored. First, the government must assign a capable coordinator who will be available to the BCA analysts. Second, more frequent progress reviews should occur to ensure the study is addressing the relevant issues and proceeding in a timely manner. Finally, all primarily affected government personnel should attend the *project definition* presentation, the *emerging results* presentation, and the *final results* presentation. If key government personnel are not available when these presentations are scheduled, then the presentations need to be rescheduled for when these government managers are available.

Using Integrated Product Teams (IPT)

Over the past decade, the practice of using IPTs has become increasingly common. The advantage of IPTs is that they typically involve members who have expertise in all, or most of, the related subject matters, as well as knowledge of the operational steps and requirements of their respective organization. Consequently, studies tend to be more balanced and comprehensive. The disadvantage of IPTs is that projects, including studies such as BCAs, tend to take much longer to complete because so many more people are involved in discussions and because it takes longer to schedule meetings (i.e., so that all the attendees can be present). However, if the BCA timeframe is flexible and the sponsoring manager considers the inclusion of all affected parties to be very important, the IPT can be often the best means.

An alternative to the IPT is to have a small core team of BCA analysts conduct research and coordinate findings as they develop. For example, analysts develop a flowchart depicting the *as-is* model, and provide it to the respective organization to ensure accuracy and completeness. This piecemeal coordination generally avoids errors of commission, and the review of early drafts precludes errors of omission. If two to six full-time analysts work on the BCA project, and they have control over their schedules, it is easier to hold them accountable to meeting the study timeline.

IPTs have advantages and disadvantages.

Skills of BCA Analysts

Study sponsors know the areas with potential for improvement. Examples include faster response time, lower emissions, higher quality, less risk, lower costs, faster turnaround time, improved technology, and so forth. Although these subject areas require someone knowledgeable about current operation and perceived requirements, this person doesn't necessarily have to be a full-time BCA analyst. This person could be a primary advisor in the respective subject area.

Not everyone with subject area knowledge should be a member of the BCA team. In most cases, specialists can be interviewed, as appropriate, and invited to attend progress reviews. These inclusions help reduce the risk that the study might miss important aspects of the operation while eliminating the need to take valued employees away from their primary jobs. Furthermore, a smaller team of analysts is nearly always preferable to a large one.[5]

If a government agency plans to adopt the practice of routinely performing BCAs, the agency may want to perform some or much of the analyses in-house. In this instance the sponsoring manager may identify an experienced government cost analyst to assist with the cost portion of the BCA. The risk of this approach is that if the agency analyst cannot, for whatever reason, perform the duties in a comprehensive and timely manner, then the team leader cannot be held accountable for the BCA.

Characteristics of Successful BCA Analysts

Attitudes and attributes oftentimes are more important than the skills one brings to the BCA. Particularly during the *preliminary research* phase of a BCA, analysts are commonly frustrated by the lack of project clarity, direction, and progress. Then during the *primary research* phase, difficulties in gathering planned data are, inevitably, encountered. Successful BCA analysts have the following characteristics:

- They are open to entirely new ideas.
- They want to learn the best practices in industry and in the government.
- They have a strong desire to improve government operations.
- They have the social skills to be effective change agents.
- They embrace the very idea of conducting such analyses.

We have found these *soft* attributes to be much more important than skills and experience in the respective subject matter area. Conversely, BCA teams that include those who are resistant to the study, frequently prevent a successful conclusion. In every BCA we have conducted, people have been resistant to the very idea of such self-critical analysis and documentation.

Oftentimes attitudes are more important than specific skills or experience.

---

[5] A BCA team consisting of five full-time analysts is nearly always more effective than one with ten part-time participants. This is because full attention can be paid to the study, and because of the nature of small groups. A five-person group generally develops an effective team working relationship more quickly than a ten-person group.

Changing Study Members During the BCA Process

Once the BCA commences, replacing analysts is especially disruptive, whether they are full time, part time, or a designated consultant. Every step possible should be taken to avoid the introduction of new team members after the BCA process is underway.

When someone new comes to the project, substantial time is required to apprise the person of all the work that has transpired and the rationale for the decisions made. Invariably, new team members want to revisit decisions made earlier in the process, and they have their own ideas as to how assumptions should be modified or how the relative weighting of the evaluation factors should be changed. In addition, because they have not been part of the discovery process, new members have difficulty contributing to discussions regarding the relative merits of each alternative. (In order to keep the BCA on schedule, issues such as these must be thoroughly addressed prior to, or at, the *project definition* decision meeting.)

Bringing new participants to the study once it is underway, disrupts the BCA process.

Implementation Team

Some BCAs are conducted to identify an optimal process for a new operation not yet in place, when an existing operation is almost certainly not the preferred solution. In these cases, the sponsoring manager may want to ensure that some personnel who have implementation responsibility are also active participants in the BCA. Personnel with implementation responsibility can teach the BCA analysts much about the inner workings of the operation being studied, the missteps, the hype versus actual results, and the experiences of others who already use the planned new process (i.e., the alternative selected). This is valuable information for those who will be involved in the creation or transfer of the government operation.

Government Contracting Personnel and the BCA

Another consideration is whether to involve government contracting personnel in some aspects of the BCA. In some instances, providing them with a copy of the final report, decision, and implementation plan makes more sense. This is sufficient for them to develop and execute contracts. In other cases the new operation is so large, complex, and so novel that it is helpful for the contracting officer to routinely attend the major decision presentations and progress reviews to fully understand the planned operation, particularly in the selection of an appropriate contract type and the development of contractual performance metrics.

For new and complex operations, personnel who have a key role in the implementation of the new process should closely follow the BCA research.

Table of Contents

While BCAs are flexible and tailored to the questions being asked, the *process* of conducting a BCA is structured and the BCA final report format is fairly standard. Our recommended table of contents is shown on the left side of the following chart. The format on the right side is the prescribed by a federal government agency, the Army Materiel Command (AMC)[6] and is shown for comparison purposes.

Recommended format	AMC format
1. Executive Summary	1. Executive Summary
2. Introduction	2. Methods and Assumptions
3. Assumptions and Methodology	A. Major Assumptions
A. Scope	B. Scope and Boundaries
B. Assumptions	C. Financial Metrics Used and Defined
C. Alternatives	D. Analysis Methodology
D. Evaluation Methodology	E. The Cost and Benefit Model
4. Operational Considerations	3. Business Impacts
5. Risks Considerations	4. Sensitivity and Risks
6. Cost Comparisons (including sensitivity analyses)	5. Conclusions and Recommendations
7. Findings	
8. Recommendations	

The reader will note the similarity of the two formats. The differences are minor and primarily one of preference.[7] What is important is to develop a sequential format that flows for the uninitiated reader. First, describe what the study addresses. Then explain the study assumptions, the alternatives evaluated, and how they are scored. The next three sections, either separate or combined, are the evaluation of the operational (or *business* or *logistics*) impacts, the risks, and the cost comparisons of the viable alternatives. Finally, assemble the results in a conclusions or *findings* section and then provide recommendations for what actions should be implemented to include a timeline and listing of required resources.

The BCA Process

A three-phased approach to the conduct of BCAs includes a *preliminary research* phase, a *primary research* phase, and a *final study* phase (see Figure 1 on page 32). These phases are, by design, distinct; that is, work on the subsequent phase does not commence until the earlier phase is complete. Chapter 4 describes in detail the goals for each of the three BCA phases.

---

[6] Guiding Principles for Performance-Based Logistics (PBL) Implementation With the U.S. Army Materiel Command (AMC), dated 29 September 2006

[7] Sensitivity analyses are a case in point. The AMC outline includes sensitivity analysis in the risk section. Presumably, the rationale is that the risk section should include a complete assessment of risks to include the risk that cost projections will be adversely affected if assumptions are altered. The reasoning for including sensitivity analysis in the cost section is that this is primarily a cost calculation, typically altering a few numbers in the formula(s) of existing spreadsheets. The obvious point is that it is far more important to properly perform sensitivity analyses than where it is included in the BCA.

Phase 1 - Preliminary Research

A BCA commences with data gathering. As a general rule, 20–30% of the total time available for the BCA should be allocated to this phase. (For example, a six-month BCA will apportion five to eight weeks for this phase.[8]) If the BCA is performed primarily by personnel familiar with the process(es) in question, the time required for preliminary research may be lessened because these personnel know the as-is model (sometimes very well) and are familiar with the improvements being sought. Still, it is typical for analysts to require some time to research alternatives, such as best practices in the government and/or industry. If the BCA team consists primarily of outside consultants, a little more time should be allocated to this phase. The preliminary research phase culminates with the *study definition* presentation and approval.

Experience has shown that having three distinct phases to the BCA works well.

Phase 2 - Primary Research

The primary research phase begins with the government sponsor's approval of the *study definition* and ends with the *emerging results* presentation. This phase typically requires 50–70% of the total BCA time available. The preponderance of data is collected, analyzed, and the findings developed during this phase. If the study is extensive, provide interim progress reports during this phase.

Phase 3 - Final Research and Documentation

Two primary activities take place during the final BCA phase: additional research that is a consequence of the *emerging results* presentation and final documentation. The time allotted for the final study phase is typically 15–25% of the total available. Often, the need for additional time develops when the *emerging results* presentation to the government sponsor results in new queries which require additional research. Also, time is needed to write the final report, prepare presentation materials, and conduct editing and proofreading. An ancillary, but important, advantage of this approach is that it provides the key decision maker with the opportunity to provide advance notice to senior leaders in the event the findings or recommendations are controversial.

---

[8] Some people advocate a longer timeline for the preliminary research phase by pointing out that it typically takes more time to document the operating steps and cost of the current system (i.e., the *as-is* model). This is true and particularly so for government operations which don't have sufficient cost accounting systems in place. While we have seen this approach work, that is, to fully research and document the as-is model before commencing the BCA or during the initial phase, we do not recommend it. Far too often this approach comes to be perceived as an exercise focused on fault finding. With such a critical orientation, more commonly than not, the entire BCA often gets canceled in its entirety.

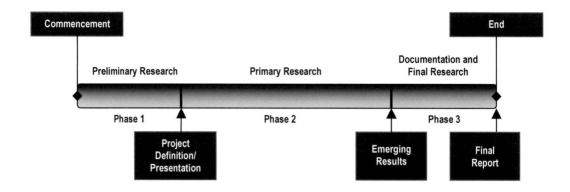

Figure 1. Three Phases of the BCA Process

Progress Reviews

Any project that requires notable resources should include interim progress reviews. A large BCA is no exception. Depending on the length of the BCA, a progress review should be provided to the study sponsor and the *advisory council* (if applicable) at an interval of every four to eight weeks. These routine progress reviews serve two primary purposes. First, they tend to assist with study discipline. When analysts get bogged down with a particular tangent or are performing their BCA functions in addition to their regular jobs, the reminder that the next progress review is upcoming often assists in maintaining the BCA schedule. The second value of progress reviews is to check on study decisions before too much time has passed. As an example, after preliminary research, analysts may conclude that a particular alternative is not viable and no further study resources will be expended to conduct additional analyses related to the alternative. This type of decision needs to be reviewed before the study proceeds for several more weeks.

Chapter 4: Commencing the Study

Executive Summary

The BCA effectively commences with key participants in a room for a three- to six-hour initial brainstorming session. When properly structured and facilitated, substantial progress can be made during this single discussion session. The initial project parameters can be developed, providing the analysts with an important understanding of where to start their research. This session also provides an important secondary advantage, in that it helps those who will be assisting with the research to gain a good understanding of the study process.

When the right attendees are present and this initial brainstorming session is conducted well, a great deal of direction can be quickly assembled. This rapid development session achieves three purposes. First, it allows the BCA analysts to hear from those who have extensive experience with the operation being evaluated. Second, it provides the analysts with insight into who has expertise for subsequent interviews. Finally, this session describes how the BCA research is expected to unfold.

Ensure Foundations are in Place

As described in chapter three, prior to commencing the BCA, the following foundational elements need to be in place:

- The general scope of the study has been identified.
- The study sponsor has been identified and is willing to participate as needed.
- The BCA team has been identified, including full-time analysts and SMEs.
- BCA project has received approval, including funding, a contract (if applicable), and key dates.
- The review and approval individual or board has been identified.

Initial Brainstorming Session

Experience has demonstrated that an initial brainstorming session with all of the key participants is an effective method of collecting key ideas and of educating ancillary participants on both what the BCA will address, as well as how the study will be conducted. If participants have ideas after they leave this meeting, they have a basic understanding as to whether their ideas will be relevant to the analysis. When they attend the *project definition* meeting and/or their opinion is sought, they will understand the context in which their expertise is contributing.

Depending on the size and complexity of the BCA, this session typically takes three to six hours. A skilled facilitator conducts the session in a room with white boards or large poster paper. This session should be conducted in an environment where (1) participants are not interrupted and (2) key personnel are present—both of these factors are paramount to the success of this session. If this initial brainstorming session needs to be rescheduled in order to have the key personnel present, this is preferable than to proceeding without them.

The initial rapid development session should cover the following areas: traditional difficulties, BCA scope, assumptions, alternatives, critical features, primary risk categories, and the evaluation method.

The BCA can achieve a significant "jump start" with a single, broadly attended and well-executed brainstorming session.

Over the course of the study, the discovery process will alter what is developed during this initial session; however, the final BCA most often retains a great deal of what is developed in this initial brainstorming session.

Step 1 – List Traditional Difficulties

Begin by listing the traditional difficulties that have been encountered with the operation.[9] Typically, government personnel have been involved in performing and/or managing this operation or process for decades and are intimately familiar with the challenges. These sessions may result in a tendency to wander off into discussions regarding why previous improvement initiatives failed or had disappointing results, and why the shortcomings are so persistent. A skilled facilitator minimizes these diversions and keeps the session to a simple listing of the traditional difficulties.

The objective of this list is twofold. First, it helps orient everyone on the facets of the operation that need improvement, and often helps lessen the resistance of those who are opposed to the very idea of conducting a BCA. Second, it assists in the subsequent step of defining the study scope.

Persistent shortcomings of the operation are often best identified by those who have been involved in the operation for decades.

Step 2 – Define the BCA Scope

The next step is to develop an initial draft of the BCA scope.[10] Defining the scope requires the full attention of those present. Oftentimes this step does not require much time, and there's a tendency to gloss over it quickly, but at every stage of the BCA the scope definition will be a focus of attention.

---

[9] It is not uncommon to encounter resistance to this listing of traditional difficulties because personnel in the room consider it to be a criticism of how they have been performing their jobs. The session facilitator should be aware of this and work to avoid the discussion becoming personal.

[10] Some texts prefer the term "study bounds" to "study scope." Either term is appropriate. For consistency, this text will use the term "scope."

Sometimes this initial scope is in the narrative form and other times it is a listing. The wording should be as specific as feasible and contain not only what is included in the study, but also specifically address what will be excluded from the study. This initial scope definition may not be the final one. At this point, the objective is to get general agreement. Participants should not spend too much time discussing minute points.

A scope that is narrow in its definition risks suboptimal solutions. That is, rather than taking an enterprise view, the study may only analyze and improve a portion of the operation, thus missing a much greater opportunity to improve the operation. A scope that is broad in its definition requires more assets (analysts and time). Also, it often requires the participation of personnel and managers from other offices or agencies, since they have responsibility for aspects of the operation being assessed. Too broad of a scope becomes very difficult to assess and more difficult to obtain approval to implement the recommendations. These can be difficult issues to decide and require considerable thought.[11]

> Too narrow a scope risks suboptimal solutions. Too broad a scope may require unacceptable time and budget resources and may risk operations outside the purview of those in the study approval decision.

During this process of developing the draft scope, returning to the list of traditional difficulties ensures the scope is capturing what is appropriate. Very often, significant discussion and decisions are required as to how to restrict or expand the scope. These are especially useful interchanges, as it is necessary for all study participants to understand the rationale and deliberate decision *not* to address every aspect of the operation in question.

> At every phase of the BCA, the scope definition will be referred to and be key to the analyses, findings, and recommendations.

Step 3 – Identify Assumptions

The next step is to identify study assumptions. When developing assumptions it is often helpful to think of explaining this operation to someone who is not familiar with it. This mental process of *stepping back* and looking at the purpose of the operation being addressed is often helpful. Like other definitions developed during this initial brainstorming session, the list of assumptions is not expected to be the final list. During the *preliminary research* phase it is not uncommon to revisit and sometimes revise the proposed assumptions.

---

[11] On occasion a BCA team may develop two draft scope statements, i.e., a broad one and a narrow one. Then the team will present these to the decision maker with the rationale for each. The scope needs to be finalized at the BCA *project definition* meeting.

These assumptions may not be evident to all participants, and those unfamiliar with the operation are often helpful when asking questions to identify the assumptions. Topics to be considered in the development of the assumptions include the following:

- What organization(s) will (continue to) have responsibility for the operation?
- What range of volume levels is assumed?
- What is the projected life of the operation or system being assessed?
- Are there restrictions or options with respect to geographical locations?
- Should the scope include statements related to resource limitations (e.g., funding, personnel)?
- Are there legal, policy, or contractual constraints which should be listed (e.g., presuming they will not change)?
- Are any reorganizations pending? If so, the impact on responsibility should be identified. If no impacts are expected, this should be explicitly stated.
- Is it appropriate to limit the impact of any changes (e.g., changes in the manner in which tax returns are processed must be transparent to the taxpayer)?
- If the BCA is required for a particular decision, this should be stated as well as the date, format, and approving authority.
- If the BCA is being conducted to achieve particular improvements (e.g., quality, turnaround time, reduction in waste, asset visibility) these should be included in the assumptions listing.

Step 4 – List Alternatives

After listing traditional difficulties, identifying a scope, and listing assumptions, the group will have developed a consensus of what the study will address. The next step is to identify the alternatives to evaluate. By convention, the first alternative is the status quo. On rare occasions there will not be a status quo (e.g., in the instance of a new operation or system being introduced to the government agency).

At least two alternatives, sometimes as many as eight or ten, are necessary.[12] The identification of alternatives can be difficult because there may not be much knowledge of best commercial practices. While government personnel will be intimately familiar with how they perform configuration management, oftentimes they do not attend conferences or work in commercial firms that manage the configuration of equipment. Consequently, uncertainty exists with respect to the alternatives that should be studied. This uncertainty is expected and should not be an obstacle at this stage of the BCA. Rather than not investigating an alternative, it is better to list all alternatives, and later eliminate them as not being viable.

In listing alternatives, consider a multitude of process, organizational, and responsibility arrangements. As an example, the choice might not be only a government-managed operation or contracting for commercially provided services). Another alternative may be a partnership arrangement where the each organization provides the aspect of the operation at which they excel.

---

[12] Some have advocated the *right* number of alternatives for a BCA, e.g., two to five. Our experience has demonstrated that the number of alternatives varies greatly depending on the complexity and breadth of the BCA, and analysts should not feel constrained to a limited number of alternatives at this point of the study.

It is much better to list all alternatives, even if they are later deemed unviable, than to miss opportunities because the team wasn't sure how applicable the commercial processes would be to the government operation.

Sometimes the team will develop close *sub-alternatives*, i.e., alternatives within an alternative. When documenting the scope, number these alternatives accordingly to assist readers. For example, the numbering of the alternatives may be 1, 2, 3(a), 3(b), and 4. Such numbering should make clear to the reader, that while five alternatives are investigated, two of them are close derivations of the other.

Step 5 – Identify Critical Features

Critical features of the operation must be identified in order for an alternative to be viable (for example, the unscheduled downtime for the hardware of an information system must be less than 0.2%). If, during the research, analysts discover that one of the alternatives will not achieve one of the listed critical features, then they can dismiss that alternative and cease further investigation. The explicit identification of these critical features assists the analysts in spending their time researching the issues that are germane to the decision. This step also helps reduce surprises at the end of the BCA when a senior manager expresses a heretofore unknown factor in what he/she considers important criteria.

The explicit identification of mandatory features increases the efficacy of the *primary research* phase and reduces the potential for surprise requirements at the end of the study.

Step 6 – Identify Primary Risk Categories

Next, identify the primary risk categories to be evaluated.[13] The objective, at this stage, is not mitigation or identifying solutions, but to help be precise in identifying all the risks. This step assists the analysts in their understanding of what types of risk to research (e.g., technical, contractual, inflationary). This discussion also provides a better understanding of how the BCA will be conducted.

---

[13] The identification of risks is included here because most BCAs include risk as one of the primary evaluation criterion. If risk is not a primary decision factor, this step can be eliminated or replaced with another consideration that is expected to have considerable weight in the final scoring.

Identify the primary risks to evaluate.

Step 7 – Determine Evaluation Methodology

The final step of this initial brainstorming session is to sketch out how the final evaluation scorecard is expected to appear. Preparing this draft scorecard requires the participants to develop their recommendations with respect to the relative importance of each of the criterion. These are beneficial discussions.

As a general rule, do not include decision criteria with a relative weighting of less than 10%. What occurs is that one of the risk factors has an overall relative weighting of 2% and the alternatives are scored as 2, 4, 3, and 5 (on a one-to-five scale). On a final scorecard, the difference between a 3 and a 4 equates to two-tenths of one percent. The fact is, in the evaluation of several objective and subjective criteria, analysts are unable to achieve accuracy anywhere in this standards-of-error range. Consequently, the BCA should not be defined in a manner that requires such precision. Table 3 depicts an example evaluation methodology.

Table 3. Evaluation Scoring

Criterion	Relative Weight	Total Possible	Alternative # 1	Alternative # 2	Alternative # 3	Alternative # 4
Safety	10%	10				
Maintenance Burden	15%	15				
Training	10%	10				
Technical Capabilities	25%	25				
Risks	10%	10				
Cost	30%	30				
		100				

While it is important to be as accurate as feasible in the projections, analysts should be careful not to imply greater precision than can be achieved when scoring subjective criterion.

At this point in the evaluation methodology, the primary emphasis should be on ideal scoring. The objective is to consider everything that is important in the decision, not only the factors for which there are easy-to-obtain objective measures. This isn't to say that issues related to data discovery should be ignored entirely, but rather that they should be secondary. If it isn't clear how the analysts determine the relative safety score, this is acceptable for the time being. Over the next few weeks, the BCA analysts will tackle the issue of how to research and apply objective scores to intangible benefits. The analysts may determine that the scoring will have to be more subjective than they'd like, or they may develop a substitute evaluation criterion for which data is available. The most important issue is a consensus on what criterion should be used to determine how each of the alternatives rank, compared to each other.

It is important to consider all the factors which are important in the decision, not just the ones for which objective measures are readily available.

The objective at this initial brainstorming session is to develop <u>initial</u> definitions of the scope, assumptions, alternatives, risks, and evaluation methodology. At this point the team should not be attempting to get these study parameters 100% final.

Chapter 5: Preliminary Research Phase

Executive Summary

The preliminary research phase typically consumes 20–30% of the total time available for the BCA. Key dates have already been identified. The purposes of this phase are to develop the initial outline of the as-is model, to determine what policies, regulatory guidance, and legal considerations are applicable, to gain a preliminary understanding of what comparable data are available, and to prepare for the *project definition* decision presentation. The *project definition* presentation should be concise, and only address the key study parameters necessary for the BCA analysts to proceed.

Preliminary Research Phase

The *preliminary research* phase typically is allocated 20–30% of the total time available for the study. The *preliminary research* phase ends with the BCA *project definition* meeting. Since the date of the *project definition* meeting has already been set, the BCA analysts should focus only on the tasks to be accomplished prior to this presentation and decision. This requires some discipline, as the initial research nearly always leads to more questions; however, the preponderance of these further research issues should be reserved for the *primary research* phase.

The objectives of the *preliminary research* phase are as follows:
- Develop a process map for the status quo (*as-is* model).
- Read and summarize applicable policies, procedures, and regulatory guidance.
- Determine what data appears to be available, and modify the evaluation methodology accordingly.
- Identify research sources for each of the alternatives.
- Conduct initial interviews, and read technical documents related to each alternative.
- Prepare for and conduct the *project definition* presentation.

Analysts should focus on validating initial plans and determining how the primary research will be conducted, rather than giving in to a temptation to delve deeper into the study issues.

Analysts should avoid trying to confirm the direction established at the initial brainstorming session. This initial direction was assembled with little or no empirical data or research, and modifications to the initial position are to be expected as more information becomes available.

A common practice is for the analysts to primarily conduct telephone interviews during the *preliminary research* phase and to rely on face-to-face interviews, which generally require travel, for the *primary research* phase. This is certainly not a prescription. The research required throughout the BCA varies greatly depending on the alternatives, the complexity of the operation, and the number of comparable practices. The great advantage of face-to-face interviews is that they often result in insights into the operation that stem from the interviewee elaborating beyond a simple response to the question posed.

Available Data and Comparison Measures

One of the intriguing aspects of the *preliminary research* phase is determining what data appears to be available. For example, the government tracks cost according to how budgets are allocated, although commercial operations use more comprehensive cost accounting systems such as Enterprise Resource Planning (ERP), Activity Based Accounting, or other cost-tracking mechanisms. The differences between systems make direct comparisons difficult. (The same phenomena are found in other data including quality, personnel systems, customer satisfaction, inventory management, and other operations.) The result is a discovery process and innovative thinking, with respect to establishing comparable metrics.

Discovery Process

The discovery process requires compromise and adaptation. Sometimes there are relatively minor differences in the manner in which the performance metric is defined (e.g., definition of "start time"), and most of the time this discovery process can be done on a sampling basis. Typically, however, the initial finding concludes that the available government data is not directly comparable to industry data; therefore, it is important to dig a little deeper to understand the differences. Sometimes it is appropriate to use measures that are standardized and/or common in an industry; however, using these measures usually requires adapting government data collection to the industry metrics that are often developed by vendors. Other times, commercial performance data is converted and adjusted to enable the analysts to compare alternatives to the known government standard metrics.

Proposed Modifications

Once study analysts determine what empirical data are available, they can propose modifications to the evaluation methodology. As an example, assume the BCA is an endeavor to reduce the total spare parts inventory holding costs. During the initial brainstorming session, the participants may have listed inventory *turn times* as a measure. However, during the *preliminary research* phase, analysts learn that while a single inventory *turn times* performance metric is used by retailers, most firms that provide spare parts use specific categories such as spare parts routinely ordered, those infrequently ordered, and parts rarely ordered. As a result, the analysts recommend that each alternative be compared according to total inventory held and *turn times* for each of three categories: spare parts ordered at least every 60 days, those ordered less frequently than once every 60 days but more often than annually, and those ordered less frequently than annually.[14] By using these data and performance metrics, comparable commercial data is available and the greater fidelity allows government managers to identify what specific improvements are available.

> One of the major objectives of the preliminary research phase is to identify what data are available and then offer suggested modifications to the initial evaluation criteria.

New information

Throughout the *preliminary research* phase, analysts need to be alert for new information which suggests the preliminary direction needs to be altered. This applies to all that was developed during the initial brainstorming session, i.e., scope, assumptions, alternatives, risks, and evaluation methodology.[15] Some of these changes are derived from data availability and some are developed during the course of learning more about the operation being studied.

In the case of a BCA to evaluate the optimal means to repair, overhaul, and return aircraft components, the initial scope was determined to include "All activities that occur at the repair depot." However, during the preliminary research phase the analysts suggested that operations related to the repair and return of crash damaged aircraft were distinctly different from those of components and scheduled aircraft overhauls. The scope of the BCA was subsequently altered to exclude distinct crash damaged aircraft processes and include only the routine components required of a typical overhaul.

Alternatives

Sometimes, during the *preliminary research* phase, analysts recommend that alternatives be deleted or combined with one another. Although combining and rewording alternatives is acceptable, making recommendations regarding the elimination of alternatives should be deferred until the *primary research* phase. Do not try to simplify the problem too quickly. As tempting as it may be, do not take preliminary findings and eliminate one of the alternatives in an effort to reduce the BCA workload. This is the *preliminary research* phase of the BCA. If the initial indications are borne out during the *primary research* phase, then is the time to recommend elimination of an alternative. As the analyst acquires more knowledge during this time, the recommendation also acquires greater credibility.

"Everything should be made as simple as possible, but not simpler." Albert Einstein

---

[14] An example might be an airplane wing spar. Although the part is infrequently ordered (i.e., only when the wing is damaged), it is still necessary to include this item in the spare parts inventory.

[15] The alert reader will note that *critical features* have been eliminated from this list. This is because the critical features were those identified by the study sponsor and are rarely modified by research.

Analysts should resist the temptation to simplify the problem too quickly.

Internal Checklist

At the completion of the *preliminary research* phase, the BCA team should pause and check their work using a checklist such as the one that follows. This checklist may also be used by the senior leader(s) reviewing progress. Of course, anytime an individual or team is held accountable to achieving such progress, the performance metrics (such as a checklist) should be provided to them in advance. A potential checklist for this internal check follows:

- ✓ Are the scope, assumptions, and alternatives clear?
- ✓ Are the alternatives consistent with the assumptions?
- ✓ Does the scope include all similar operations?
- ✓ If the scope is intentionally limited (e.g., a pilot program), is the rationale provided?
- ✓ Has the study methodology been fully described, and is there concurrence by all who will review the final results?
- ✓ Does the BCA team of analysts consist of people with the right skills and temperament?
- ✓ Will the cost section only compare the BCA alternatives or will the cost analyses be formatted and researched to meet other requirements also?
- ✓ Is there valid and attainable data for the planned comparison of alternatives?
- ✓ Is a BCA the best analytical tool (i.e., instead of a cost analysis or process redesign)?
- ✓ What are the major improvements anticipated?
- ✓ What resources are planned for this BCA?
- ✓ Is the amount of time allocated for this BCA the right amount?
- ✓ Who is the study sponsor? Will he/she actively participate as required?
- ✓ Is an advisory group appropriate for this BCA? If yes, are the right members assembled?
- ✓ Does it appear that pursuing improvements in the area defined by the scope will result in sub-optimized solutions, e.g., saving money or other improvements here but at the expense of transferring workload elsewhere?
- ✓ Are there BCAs, cost analyses, logistical studies, or other research with data, findings, or conclusions that can be used in this BCA?
- ✓ Is the timeline (Gantt schedule) for the remainder of the BCA well established?
- ✓ Are the available travel funds consistent with the research tasks?

Preparing for the Project Definition Presentation

The *preliminary research* phase culminates with the *project definition* presentation. Analysts should keep in mind that they will be presenting *recommendations,* only, to the decision maker(s). Analysts do not decide what should be studied or on what basis the study decision should be made. These decisions are the responsibility of the study sponsor or BCA review council, if applicable.

Decisions with respect to what should be studied and on what basis the alternatives should be compared belong solely with the study sponsor.

Provide a Read-ahead Summary

The *project definition* presentation should be focused. This is not the time to impress participants with how much research has been conducted nor speculate on where the study results may lead. Depending on the preference of the study sponsor, a read-ahead package of the discussion topics may be advisable—especially if the presentation is to a BCA board or council.

If senior managers are attending the project definition meeting, each of them should receive a read-ahead summary of what will be discussed. They should receive these five to ten days prior to the meeting. This practice tends to greatly facilitate the effectiveness of the presentation and discussions.

Recommended Presentation Sequence

To reiterate, the *project definition* presentation should be concise. Limit the presentation and discussion to key issues. If there are more than twenty charts planned for the presentation there may be another agenda. A recommended presentation sequence follows:

- Chart # 1 – Why Conduct This BCA?
  The introduction chart should provide a review of why this study is being conducted; i.e., who chartered the study? If there is an external requirement, state this. If the BCA is being conducted primarily to identify the optimal means to achieve improvements, this should be clearly stated. The presenter should pause and give the study sponsor an opportunity to clarify the wording of this purpose statement.

- Chart # 2 – Introduce the BCA Team
  The full-time, on-call analysts working on the study should be present and introduced. Effective meeting protocol calls for everyone in the room to be introduced. If there are any potentially affected organizations that are not represented, but were invited, the study sponsor should be notified so that he/she can decide whether to proceed with the presentation or reschedule it.

All personnel who have a voice in the review and approval of the final BCA should be present at the project definition presentation.

- Chart # 3 – BCA Timeline
  The basis timeline for the overall BCA should be provided. Only key dates are typically required, i.e., when the study commenced, the initial brainstorming session, project definition presentation, emerging results, and final report. Depicting the three phases with the presentations which define them is often helpful.

- Chart # 4 – BCA Scope
  The proposed scope of the BCA should be provided. Sometimes this is in a narrative form of one to three sentences, and sometimes it is a list. Remember to include both what is included, as well as that which is specifically excluded from the planned study.

Each briefing point, or chart, should be modified in accordance with the direction of the study sponsor(s).

- Chart # 5 – BCA Assumptions
  List the study assumptions. Provide ample time for discussion of the assumptions. It may be helpful to point out to the study sponsor that problematic challenges to BCA results are more often associated with study assumptions than any other aspect. Before leaving this chart, the decision maker(s) should be very comfortable with the stated assumptions. If alterations in the assumptions are needed, making them now is the appropriate time.

Challenges to well conducted, complete BCAs are much more often associated with the study assumptions or evaluation methodology than they are with the underlying support data.

- Chart # 6 – Alternatives
  List and describe each of the alternatives that will be studied and assessed. While the specific descriptions of how some alternatives will work may not yet be fully known, the BCA team leader should be able to articulate the currently known *idea* as to how each alternative would work. If further questions are asked regarding more detailed descriptions, the response is that more details will be developed during the *primary research* phase. The study sponsor may

elect to expand the alternatives or eliminate one or more entirely, and should be encouraged to make such decisions at this point. If the sponsor has reasons for being unwilling to implement one of the alternatives, then identifying these reasons now allows the study analysts to dedicate their attention to the alternatives which will be considered.

- Chart # 7 – Critical Features
Although this list has previously been provided by the study sponsor, this is an excellent time to review it. If the recipients of the presentation are a BCA council, there may be discussion of this list. Oftentimes there are also slight modifications to the wording of the critical features in order to clarify the intent, without eliminating viable alternatives by adhering to the *letter of the law* too closely.

- Chart # 8 – Primary Risk Categories
The BCA team leader should list the primary risk categories that will be studied. Since preliminary research has been completed, oftentimes this listing can be elaborated at this point with subcategories.

Throughout the *project definition* presentation, the BCA team leader should present draft points and be active in soliciting comments to modify those points.

- Chart # 9 – Evaluation Relative Weights
The BCA team leader should ask the study sponsor for a preference with respect to the relative weighting of the decision criteria. Provide a list, and ask the decision maker to apply a percentage next to each of the evaluation criteria (e.g., risk, retention of key skills, cost, technical capabilities, and maintenance support). Experience has shown that it is preferable *not* to provide the study sponsor with recommendations. It is important to reinforce to the study sponsor, as well as the BCA analysts, that this assessment is to provide information that allows the study sponsor to make a comparison and decision. With respect to the allocation of the percentage applied to each evaluation criterion, no standard answer exists. The correct answer is what the study sponsor deems important.

Study sponsors who make greater contributions to the *project definition* presentation take greater ownership in the BCA.

- Chart # 10 – Summary

   The purpose of this meeting is for the study sponsor to determine the key parameters of the study. All comments and suggested changes are welcome at this point, but after the participants leave the room, the *primary research* phase begins. This is similar to the architect telling the prospective homeowners that they can make any changes they'd like today; however, if they approve the plans, they should know that the cement trucks are coming tomorrow. Any changes in the BCA definition after this point will either require more resources, including time, or reduce the detail in which the study can be performed and, consequently, the credibility of the BCA. If there are any remaining open issues to be decided they should be identified now. Open issues of any significance should delay commencement of the *primary research* phase.

At the final review of the house drawings the architect reminds the prospective homeowners that any changes after today will be much more expensive and delay completion of construction.

Criticality of the Agreement on the Project Definition

The BCA team lead should go to great lengths to ensure that all who will have a voice at the end are present in the room on the day of this presentation. The importance of having the key decision makers present and having their agreement cannot be overemphasized.

In one instance, a two-year study occurred at an estimated cost of $800,000. When the alternative was selected, another government agency disagreed because of the negative repercussions the decision would have on them. After another six months of senior-level discussions and meetings, the final decision was to not implement the planned change. A decision as to what should have been considered in the evaluation of the alternatives should have occurred early in the study, before the expensive and time consuming *primary research* occurred.

Project Definition Documentation

Decisions made at the *project definition* presentation must be documented. If the BCA has a limited scope and the study sponsor is the only one affected, this can often be accomplished by revising the *project definition* charts to reflect the revisions. If there are substantive changes and the BCA team leader anticipates the final results may be controversial, the *project definition* decisions may be placed in a separate document. In some instances, it may take days or even weeks after the *project definition* presentation to resolve differences and arrive at a decision. If the BCA is complex and crosses the boundaries of other organizations or agencies, the team leader should distribute and collect a signature page which confirms that the participants agree on what will be studied and how the alternatives will be evaluated.

An essential step in the BCA process is documentation that all agree reflects the decisions made in conjunction with the *project definition* presentation.

Chapter 6: Primary Research Phase

Executive Summary

During the *primary research* phase, the preponderance of research occurs and the findings developed. Topics typically included are various sections such as technical, operational, risk, and cost. The research and analyses needs to be consistent with the study parameters finalized at the *project definition* presentation, or shortly thereafter. Scoring for each of the sections and each alternative needs to be consistent. The final scorecard should be formatted in the manner determined at the *project definition* presentation. At the end of the *primary research* phase, the team should also assemble the study ancillary findings. These are a compilation of the observations which are not directly relevant to the BCA itself, but were discovered during the study and may be helpful information to the study sponsor. The *primary research* phase culminates in the *emerging results* presentation. The purpose of the *emerging results* presentation is to learn of any additional research that is needed and to provide the decision maker(s) with notice of potentially controversial findings.

Introduction

The *primary research* phase requires the skills of various analysts, as well as an effective team leader. During this phase the preponderance of research occurs and findings developed. Although there is a tendency for analysts to look ahead to this phase during the *preliminary research* phase, an effective BCA team leader understands that the successful completion of all three phases is essential to a successful study, and limits this tendency. After all, until the *project definition* presentation, no decision on *what* to study has been made. Analysts must not proceed to the *primary research* phase until decisions have been discussed and finalized.

The melding of the various elements during this discovery period requires frequent discussions and constant coordination between the technical analysts, logisticians, risk analysts, cost accountants, and other team members. An effective and experienced team leader ensures that while the study team members work independently, they also closely coordinate activities and findings. As one analyst begins pursuing a lead, the others are apprised of developments and may elect to join in the research.

The analysts need to strike the right balance between being open to entirely new and applicable practices, and the need to complete the BCA within the provided timeline. If a moderate amount of research indicates that a particular alternative is not viable, document this discovery so that no further research relative to this alternative occurs. A combination of adaptability[16] and focus on the timely identification of findings for the *emerging results* presentation is crucial.

---

[16] As a practical note, if the BCA team consists of contractors, the government contracting officer should anticipate contract modifications to adjust for the unknowns. As an example, some travel may not be needed and the funds should be transferred to one of the labor categories. This is a research project and the government should not expect that all the required resource information will be known at the beginning of the study.

The BCA team typically consists of specialists. For example, assume the purpose of the study is to determine the optimal means to overhaul and repair turbine engines. The team may consist of the following full time members:

- Team Lead – Someone who has participated on several BCAs
- Senior Maintenance Technician – Someone who thoroughly understands the depot maintenance requirements and processes
- Mid Level Supply Specialist – Someone knowledgeable in how the engines are packaged for shipment, stored, tracked, and moved to and from the repair depot
- Senior Cost Analyst – Someone experienced in cost analyses, particularly where comparable data sources were difficult to identify
- Apprentice Analyst – A junior level analyst (i.e., first or second BCA) who assists with coordination and assigned tasks
- The team may have additional part-time staffing, e.g., an administrative assistant at 30% workload and 80 hours for report editing.

In this example, the team may also elect to visit Delta Airlines and the Union Pacific Railroad[17] to learn how they overhaul and repair turbine engines, what performance metrics they use, transportation and tracking means, and what costs are incurred. The entire team should participate in such visits. During breaks, lunchtime, and discussions over dinner each analyst is able to provide observations that assist the others in the discovery process.

 Sometimes surprisingly insightful comments come from those with the least experience with the current operation. It is important to establish a discussion atmosphere that is conducive to soliciting the views of all the team members.

Developing a Research Plan

Armed with the expertise of each of the analysts, the knowledge gained during the *preliminary research* phase, and the outcome of the *project definition* presentation, the team leader has the requisite information to develop the research plan.

A useful guideline is that the amount of time spent on a topic should be somewhat commensurate with the relative weighting of the evaluation criteria. For example, if quality accounts for 10% of the evaluation criterion, then approximately 10% of the analyst's time should be allocated to researching and documenting the quality differences between each alternative. This is a *general* guideline regarding the allocation of research resources; do not adhere to it too closely.

---

[17] Experience has shown that commercial firms are generally open to hosting such benchmarking visits. They are proud of their accomplishments and this is an opportunity to show what they've done. Also, as citizens, they are interested in assisting the government in becoming more efficient.

More research sources result in higher confidence in the projections and greater credibility of the findings and recommendations; however, this confidence is achieved by committing more time and money. Tradeoffs are inevitable.

Finalizing the Scorecard

Within the first few weeks of the primary research phase, the BCA team should finalize its internal scorecard format. Developing this detailed, internal scorecard requires excellent judgment. To compare quality across the alternatives being evaluated, the team may develop five sub-factors to score. Examples might be the rework rate, documentation, quality procedures, number of personnel trained or certified in quality procedures, and the frequency and effectiveness of variance analyses. If the evaluation methodology finalized at the *project definition* presentation has six major categories, the BCA team may have thirty or forty elements to score.

Advantages of Using a Large Number of Scoring Factors

The advantage in having a higher number of factors scored is threefold:

1. By developing scores for a large number of factors, the overall credibility of the findings is enhanced because the discovery process was wide ranging.
2. More data points reflect either overall trends or strengths and weaknesses distributed throughout the alternatives.[18]
3. Often overlooked is the advantage that a large number of sub-factors results in less dissention by those who don't like the findings. Because of the large number of other factors, an individual score won't matter that much.

Using the example above, assume the government repair depot manager disliked receiving a lower evaluation than one of the commercial outsourcing alternatives. It is immediately apparent that arguing that his depot should have received a rating of three on rework rate rather than the two that the BCA analyst gave him will have no discernable effect on the overall outcome. The re-work rate sub-factor accounted for one fifth of the quality score which has a 10% weight in the overall evaluation criterion. Consequently, if he succeeds in persuading the analysts to increase his rework rate score from a two to a three, the overall rating for the depot will increase by 0.4%. Rarely is this enough to make a difference in the overall findings.

---

[18] This is often valuable information for the decision maker. As an example, if alternative # 2 and # 4 are nearly tied, and the study sponsor is aware of recent quality improvement initiatives, this information will assist in making the selection.

A significant advantage to scoring a large number of sub-factors is that it reduces the dissention if the findings are not what some prefer.

Disadvantages of Using a Large Number of Scoring Factors

The obvious disadvantage to designing an internal scorecard with many sub-factors is that greater complexity results in more work, although this increased workload is not as substantial as it may initially appear. In many instances it simply means asking more questions during site visits.

The questions asked during the research of each alternative need to be consistent.

Site Visits and Scoring

The research plan may include site visits because the greater the sampling, and the more data elements evaluated, the greater the accuracy, certainty, and eventual credibility of the BCA. Analysts struggle with evaluating that which is important and documenting empirical data which can be audited and replicated.

Analysts will encounter sites that are dirty, where performance metrics are outdated and not being used, or there seems to be an overall lack of professionalism. At other sites they'll encounter conscientious, enthusiastic workers and managers with disciplined procedures and an obvious desire to excel. While these can, and should, be important characteristics to differentiate one alternative from another, it is exceedingly difficult to apply objective measures to these subjective aspects. This difficulty can be resolved by a combination of scoring all that is important (even when the scores are more subjectively determined) and incorporating such information in the final recommendations. Frequently, more objective data can be achieved by the creation of additional sub-metrics.[19]

---

[19] As an example, when one observes an organization with high morale and high performing employees versus another with high turnover and seemingly poor dedication, this can be documented with the organization's human resource practices.

 People typically have a strong preference for objective measures over subjective evaluations. This doesn't mean they're more important. The BCA should include assessments of all that is important to determining the optimal solution.

Operational Impacts[20]

The broad term *operational impacts* is used here in lieu of a variety of more specific categories for this section. Depending on the BCA topic, this section could use any of the following titles: organizational impacts, technical considerations, business operations, customer service, supply chain management, logistics, and so forth.

Frequently, this category accounts for 50–70% of the overall BCA evaluation criteria. Because of this importance, sub-factors should be prepared for this category. Examples of such sub-factors include the following:

- Responsibilities and requirements of government managers
- Retention of critical skills within the government agency and/or personnel
- Technical innovation rates
- Access to best practices and/or state-of-the-art equipment, technology, or processes
- Inventory levels and management practices
- Configuration management
- Legal considerations
- Policy guidance and adherence
- Experience performing this function, or a similar one
- An enterprise solution rather than sub-optimal piecemeal responsibilities
- Quality control and quality assurance
- Database access, accuracy, control, and/or enterprise data interchange
- Organizational structure and responsibilities
- The ability to ensure (enforce) performance objectives are achieved
- Visibility into the operation
- The ability to adapt to required or desired changes quickly

---

[20] The reader may ask why this section of the BCA, which is typically the most heavily weighted portion of the evaluation criterion, receives scant attention in this guide. The topics covered in a BCA range from determining the optimal means of maintaining air traffic control equipment to the best means of disposing of excess commercial construction cranes the Army has deployed overseas. With such a wide variety of potential subjects, it is impossible to provide specific how-to guidance in this section. Further, it is hoped that the general guidance provided throughout this text (e.g., using three distinct phases, the selection of the BCA team leader, developing the evaluation criterion and format) are sufficient to provide effective leaders with the framework in which to establish specific procedural steps and metrics applicable to the particular BCA scope.

 If the relative evaluation rating for operational impacts is 50–70%, then score the sub-factors as well. Each of these sub-categories may have three to seven assessment questions used to develop and document the supporting rationale for the score.

Risks

One of the major categories considered in the BCA should be risk. In practically every study, the alternatives vary with respect to risk. Depending on the preferences of the study sponsor, risk may account for as little as 10% of the overall decision criteria or as much as 30%. If risk accounts for 10% of a BCA and there are five risk sub-categories, then each of the risk sub-categories would account for 2% of the overall score.[21] Risk is generally analyzed within the government to determine mitigation strategies; however, this is not the intent of the BCA risk section. The BCA process identifies the risk and evaluates its projected importance.

BCA analysts need to be alert to risks which have the potential to eliminate an alternative. These are typically risks that have the possibility of a major impact such as a substantial delay, cost overruns, or loss of life. Sometimes it is appropriate to advocate the elimination of one of the alternatives due to the risk associated with it. That is, even though the risk score is such that it won't appreciably affect the selection of an alternative, a high risk probability and consequence may be such that the decision maker should be apprised of recommendations to avoid this alternative, regardless of the score.

 Sometimes it is appropriate to recommend elimination of an alternative due to the high risk associated with a particular aspect. This may be contrary to the predetermined evaluation methodology but so significant that it needs to be brought to the attention of the decision maker.

Risk Categories

The number of risk categories and the types of risks evaluated depends on the BCA. The following, partial list of risks should generate ideas about risk.[22] The list is not inclusive of all the risks that might be applicable, nor would all these risks be present in a single BCA.

---

[21] Generally the BCA time and resource constraints are such that one doesn't want to research, score, and document factors that account for less than 1% or 2% of the total BCA score.

[22] The very notion of being able to identify the risks associated with an endeavor warrants a book in itself. For an excellent text on this subject the reader should consider <u>The Black Swan</u> by Nassim Nicholas Taleb. However, as a practical matter, the fact that people aren't very good at identifying infrequent but highly impactful risks doesn't negate the value of engaging in the sort of risk analyses discussed in this text.

Operational or Technical Maturity – Some alternatives are processes, operations, and procedures that have been performed for several years. In these instances there is less risk than for those operations that are in their *beta* testing stage or have only been demonstrated at one or two sites.

Course Reversal – What are the consequences if an alternative is selected and it doesn't work? How difficult and/or expensive and time consuming will it be to un-do the implementation decision?

Responsibility and Authority Alignment – Some alternatives have structures in which there is poor alignment of responsibility with authority. Some have complex arrangements where one government entity is responsible for one aspect of the operation, a commercial firm has another portion, and another government agency or commercial firm has responsibility for another. There is a greater risk of performance, schedule, and cost variance with multiple managers than organizational arrangements using a single manager with clear lines of authority.[23]

Personnel Qualifications – Alternatives often vary with respect to the likelihood (or demonstrated track record) of being able to provide qualified personnel to perform the work. Some alternatives are likely to be more capable and responsive in the hiring of personnel when needed and/or the termination of poor performing employees. Often there are applicable certification standards such as ISO, FAA, CPA and others which will aid the analyst in documenting personnel qualifications.

Contractual Issues – The government has ample examples where managers and contracting officers believe they were clear in the contractual requirements but issues arose during performance that created problems. What level of confidence exists that the stated requirements in the contract will be performed at the cost, quality, and timeliness expected?

Typically some alternatives will have greater risk than others. It's important that this risk be identified and considered in the evaluation.

Performance – There are instances in which the government has experience with a provider being considered in one of the alternatives. This may be a contractor or a government organization with whom it has been difficult to work with or who routinely misses contractual requirements or commitments.

Transition – Relocating existing support from one organization to another nearly always entails some transition risk. Some equipment may not be identified and moved. Personnel expertise will not be complete at the new location on day one. Typically, there are procedures which are known

---

[23] Note that the risk section is <u>not</u> where the alternatives should be scored with respect to higher or lower government workload to manage the operation or portions of the operation. These performance-related issues (i.e., advantages and disadvantages) should be addressed in the operational impacts section of the BCA.

by current operators but undocumented. Some commercial firms have little experience working with the government and encounter difficulties with contractual reporting or other procedural requirements. Since there is no transition with the status quo, this alternative generally receives the best scores in this sub-category.

Business Longevity – When evaluating the likelihood that the provider will remain in existence during the planned period, there may be differences with respect to risk. Very rarely do government organizations cease to exist. It is exceedingly unusual for large companies to declare bankruptcy and go out of business during the course of a contract but it does occur. The probability that a small company might lose key contracts or key executives may be a risk that should be considered.

Management Experience & Expertise – Frequently some alternatives will have managers who are familiar with the operation in question and have effectively managed either this particular process or one similar in complexity and size. While selecting an alternative without this track record or experienced managers in place may be the optimal choice, the higher risk of doing so should be recognized.

Technical Expertise – The operation(s) may require specialized expertise, specialized facilities, test equipment, tooling, database, parts marking,[24] or other technical capabilities. It may be appropriate to assess the risk of one alternative versus another with respect to technical capabilities.

Funding Adaptability – Some government programs are notorious for funding variances. The agency may receive congressional plus-ups or short notice funding decrements. When this occurs, how responsive will the provider be to changing their volume, rates of production, or other deliverables in accordance with changes in government funding?[25]

Asking the decision maker to allocate the relative evaluation criteria at the *project definition* presentation helps ensure that risks are not given too much, nor too little, consideration.

Cost Controls – Some organizations (alternatives) will have mature and robust cost controls in place. These include government approved cost accounting systems, active use of Earned Value Management System (EVMS) progress tracking, disciplined procedures for billing, and daily or even hourly visibility into cost incurred. Other organizations (frequently, the government) will not have detailed cost accounting systems and disciplined procedures in place and, hence, there will be greater risk that budgeted cost will be exceeded and/or it may take considerable time before cost overruns are recognized, reported, and corrective action can take place.

---

[24] The DoD requirement for Unique Identification (UID) parts marking is an example. Developing this capability is more difficult, expensive, and time consuming than is often assumed.
[25] Note: this is not a risk of funding variation. While this risk may occur, it will be the same for all the alternatives. This risk is how adaptable each alternative is expected to be when (if) this occurs.

Innovation – Organizations vary with respect to how well they adapt to process redesign such as ISO 9000 certification, process layouts, software upgrades, data and document management, implementing tracing and tracking technology, and personnel upgrade training. If the alternative selected entails the requirement for substantial changes, it may be appropriate to project the risk that each organization will have in adopting the new processes.

Unknown – Some alternatives entail greater change and, consequently, will include some unknowns that are not present in continuing to perform the operation in the same manner, by the same personnel, at the same location. The more radical the change being proposed, the more likely there will be some facets of the operation which will be overlooked.[26]

Some risk analysts refer to unknown risks at the "unknown unknowns."

To reiterate, this is not an exhaustive list of risk sub-categories that might be included in a BCA. Rather, it is provided to serve as example and a catalyst for discussions regarding which risks are appropriate to identify and evaluate.

Objectivity

One of the most difficult areas in risk calculation is objectivity. To calculate a true statistical risk, use the number of failures and successes. For example, if there were 29 programs and 18 were deemed successful the result is a 62% success rate.

The problem with this type of model is the lack of failure data. Organizations rarely track failure data per se, and when they do have it they are especially protective of this data.[27] Organizations and more specifically, managers, focus on success. Even if an analyst was fortunate enough to collect this type of data, it would be rare to have comparable data for each alternative.[28] This type of "empirical" data can also have a large number of variables which are not addressed. The human desire for concrete data can result in unwarranted credibility to this type of result.

---

[26] Some BCA analysts prefer to consider transition risks and unknown risks in the same sub-category.

[27] One encounters commercial operations where past failures are documented and studied. Healthy companies will have stories about failures. Firms operate in a competitive environment their very survival is often at stake. Commercial entities have a strong incentive to avoid replicating expensive errors. Conversely, this documented, critical self assessment is rarely practiced in the government (the exception being military operations).

[28] This is a habitual logic error found in business books. Research will reflect that "…68% of the most profitable companies utilize Enterprise Resource Planning (ERP) systems." In order to provide valid and useful information, the question needs to be asked: How many unsuccessful companies use(d) ERP systems?

Successes are remembered and touted while failures are quickly forgotten.

Double-Counting

In deciding which risks to include and score, analysts need to be careful not to double count. For example, analysts evaluating capabilities in the operational section may downgrade one alternative because the organization doesn't have documented processes in place. Since this shortcoming may adversely affect scores in the risk section, this alternative has a higher risk of performance due to the absence of mature process documentation. In this example, this shortcoming should be addressed in the operational section of the BCA and not re-addressed in the risk section. Naturally, this delineation needs to be fully explained at the *emerging results* presentation and in the final report.

Take care to avoid including a single shortcoming in more than one section. To do so will result in double counting and most likely be inconsistent with the established evaluation methodology.

Scoring Risk

Scoring in the BCA should be consistent throughout, with higher scores desirable. However, a higher risk score is generally deemed as undesirable. That is, a high score implies there is high risk. Therefore, it is necessary to clearly state the scoring method used for risk in the BCA. For example, a final scorecard may look like the one depicted below.

BCA Final Scorecard

Note: Ratings are 1 to 5 with 1 being the lowest and 5 being the highest.

Criterion	Relative Weight	Alternative # 1		Alternative # 2		Alternative # 3	
		Raw Score	Weighted Score	Raw Score	Weighted Score	Raw Score	Weighted Score
Technical	15%	4	12%	3	9%	5	15%
Logistics	50%	3	30%	5	50%	4	40%
Risk	10%	2	4%	3	6%	3	6%
Cost	25%	4	20%	3	15%	2	10%
	100%		66%		80%		71%

While a low risk is desirable, a high score is preferable. Consequently, for the sake of clarity and overall consistency it is better to reverse the risk scores. That is, a risk score of one is a high risk, and a score of five is low risk. This is counterintuitive to those who routinely perform risk analyses.[29]

In the final report, use consistent scoring and provide results on a percent scale. Readers are accustomed to this format and its use reduces misunderstandings.

Keeping Risk in Context

The risk of an endeavor is measured by its projected consequence and the probability of the event occurring. When assigning risk in the BCA, the overall endeavor needs to be kept in context. If the operation being studied is expected to have annual production rates of 2,500 components and cost a million dollars, then an outcome that results in annual production of 1,000 units at a cost of $1.5M will likely be evaluated as a high risk. However, to those who consider risk in endeavors which have the potential to result in the loss of life, this will not seem like a high risk. But this is the point: risk evaluations should be commensurate with the operation being assessed, and, to this end, the scoring consequences should be defined. An example is provided in the illustration below.

Scoring Consequences
(Sample only)

Level	Technical Performance	Schedule	Cost
1	Minimal or no consequence to technical performance	Minimal or no impact	Minimal or no impact
2	Minor reduction in technical performance or supportability, can be tolerated with little or no impact on program	Able to meet key dates. **Slip < 6 weeks**	Budget increase or unit production cost increases. **< 1% of Budget**
3	Moderate reduction in technical performance or supportability with limited impact on program objectives	Minor schedule slip. Able to meet key milestones with no schedule float. **Slip < 3 months**	Budget increase or unit production cost increase **< 5% of Budget**
4	Significant degradation in technical performance or major shortfall in supportability; may jeopardize program success	Program critical path affected. **Slip < 6 months**	Budget increase or unit production cost increase **< 10% of Budget**
5	Severe degradation in technical performance; Cannot meet key technical/supportability threshold; will jeopardize program success	Cannot meet key program milestones. **Slip > 6 months**	Exceeds APB threshold **> 10% of Budget**

---

[29] This will also be true in the evaluation of cost where low cost will receive a high score.

There may be identified risks with some aspect of one of the alternatives but mitigation plans are in place, and the study analysts are persuaded that they will be effective in lessening the risk.[30] When this belief affects the risk score applied, it should be clearly stated. As an example, there may be concerns that a commercial firm does not have sufficient capacity to meet peak demand, but this has been addressed by plans to qualify a subcontractor.

> If the risk score applied includes an assumption that certain risk mitigation steps will be successful, this should be clearly stated.

The scoring means used to determine the likelihood of an event occurring should also be clearly stated. An example is illustrated below:

Risk Level	Likelihood	Probability of Occurrence
1	Highly Unlikely	< 1%
2	Not Likely	2 – 5%
3	Possible	6 - 20%
4	Likely	21 – 49%
5	Probable	> 50%

> An additional advantage of providing the rationale for all scoring is that it is easy to alter the scoring methodology and perform what-if calculations, e.g., relative weighting or severity of outcome.

Scoring Consequences

The risk scoring method should also describe the consequences. An example is reflected below.[31]

---

[30] When risk is identified, there are four alternatives for the manager, i.e., to accept it, mitigate the risk, transfer it, or avoid the activity.

[31] This is just an example. These descriptions would vary depending on the size and complexity of the operation.

Severity of Outcome	Description
1	Schedule slippage of two weeks or less. Cost increases of < 2%. No adverse publicity. No reductions in quality or performance.
2	Schedule slip of 2–6 weeks. Cost increases of 3–6%. No decrease in quality or performance outcomes.
3	Schedule slip of 6–12 weeks. Cost increases of 7–10%. Slight adverse publicity. Quality or performance reductions of 5–10%.
4	Schedule delays of 3–6 months. Cost increases of 11–15%. Notable quality or performance reductions (i.e., 10–25%).
5	Schedule delays of >6 months. Cost increases of >15%. Substantial quality or performance degradation.

Risk Reporting Matrix

The conventional means by which risk is illustrated is a risk reporting matrix. A sample is illustrated below.

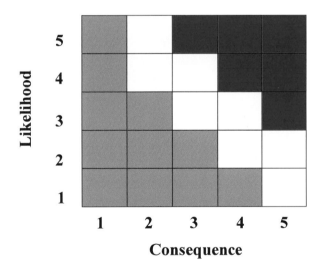

The green blocks are deemed to be low risk (acceptable), the yellow blocks are categorized as moderate risks, and the red ones as high risk (unacceptable). The assignment of these colors is determined by the BCA analysts and can be easily altered if key decision makers have preferences for different labels.

While the scoring of risk for sub-categories is fairly straight-forward (as described in the previous pages), the difficulties of evaluating risk for the BCA as a whole are threefold:

1. Combining the risks into a single evaluation
2. Avoiding obscuring important risk considerations by averaging or other merging
3. Converting the risk reporting matrix information into a score

Meet the first challenge by not merging the various risks into a single rating. For example, assume the BCA evaluated five risk sub-categories: performance, transition, course reversal, cost controls, and unknowns. In this case, each of these sub-categories should stand alone as separate risks to be considered in the selection of the optimal alternative. Each should be presented to the decision maker and each should be documented in the study without combining it with another.

A fair amount of unavoidable subjectivity exists in the identification and scoring of risks. If notable risks exist in a particular sub-category, the report should highlight these categories for special attention, in case the pre-determined evaluation methodology does not adequately convey the important decision criteria to the study sponsor.

To meet the second challenge, avoid the error of combining evaluations or use averaging. The result of these actions can be to inadvertently obscure risk considerations when numbers are applied to the consequences and likelihood of several different risk sub-categories and then, in an effort to simplify the results, these evaluations are merged into a single score. For example, one sub-category might have a high risk due to the risk being of moderate likelihood and a severe consequence. If this high risk score of "2" is then combined with other scores, the fact that one of the alternatives has a risk will not be evident to the decision maker.

BCA analysts need to be careful that, in the interest of simplicity or presentation concerns, they don't obscure important risk considerations.

Meet the third challenge by converting the risk reporting matrix evaluations into numerical scores that can be included in the overall comparison of alternatives. One conversion method is to include the separate scores on an equal basis. This might be depicted as follows:

Risk Scoring								

Note: Ratings are 1 to 5 with 1 being the lowest and 5 being the highest.

		Alternative # 1		Alternative # 2		Alternative # 3	
Risks	*Relative Weight*	*Raw Score*	*Weighted Score*	*Raw Score*	*Weighted Score*	*Raw Score*	*Weighted Score*
Performance	20%	4	16%	3	12%	4	16%
Transition	20%	5	20%	2	8%	3	12%
Course Reversal	20%	3	12%	5	20%	4	16%
Cost Controls	20%	2	8%	2	8%	4	16%
Unknowns	20%	5	20%	2	8%	3	12%
	100%		76%		56%		72%

Weighting Risk Sub-categories

An argument exists for altering the relative weighting of risk sub-categories when some risks may be more important than others. The problem with this approach is that the BCA will appear to have greater accuracy than exists. In the previous example, the "course reversal" risk is weighted at 20% of overall risk which (assume) has a 10% weighting in the overall evaluation criteria. This means that the "course reversal" risk will account for 2% of the final scoring. Altering the relative weights of these five risk sub-categories would result in evaluations that accounted for 1% or 1.5% of the total. No BCA will ever be this accurate, i.e., to provide final scoring that is accurate to ± 2%. While the overall BCA has some subjective evaluations, the risk section in particular, tends to be more subjective. If the study team leader elects to score sub-categories that account for less than 5% of the overall scoring, the decision maker should clearly understand that this level of detail should not be construed as implying this level of accuracy.

The BCA invariably includes some conversion of subjective evaluations to objective scores. Be careful not to convey a greater level of accuracy in the projections (i.e., of one alternative over another) than exists.

Cost Evaluations

Most government agencies have extensive experience in performing cost analyses and many have prescribed cost methodologies. Cost analyses may be performed by a separate group or all cost analyses conducted will have to be validated by the cost analyses group in accordance with the listing of costs to be included and a prescribed format. If this is the case, the reader can skip this section.

BCA team members should meet with the applicable government cost analysts who will prepare or approve cost analyses and prepare this section according to their guidelines.

 If the government agency has established processes for the preparation or approval of cost analyses, then the BCA analysts need to comply with these procedures.

The cost section of the BCA report commonly receives more scrutiny than any other aspect. This is despite the fact that cost may account for 20–30% of the evaluation criteria. The reason for this is that cost is familiar and the data objective.

 People like to focus on factors they understand well. A result might be that, although cost might account for 25% of a BCA, 50–70% of the time can be spent gathering and explaining cost data.

Defining Cost

The first and preeminent question is what aspects of cost will be researched, collected, analyzed, and included? Oftentimes there is a tendency to define the BCA such that the cost section will not only answer the questions relative to the projected cost of each alternative, but will also serve other purposes. There may be a desire for the cost section to be complete enough that it will enable managers to submit budget requests after the selected alternative is identified. It is also common for managers to want to use the BCA cost section as a should-cost analysis or a Life Cycle Cost Estimate (LCCE).[32] These important decisions need to be clarified at the *project definition* presentation.

Single Purpose for Cost Evaluations

Try to avoid having the BCA cost projections serve multiple functions. The reason is because each of the various cost estimates is structured to answer specific questions. As stated earlier, identifying and collecting comparable data is challenging. Good cost analysts will have to be creative in finding and documenting comparable empirical and/or parametric data. The primary question in the BCA is what is the relative cost of each alternative? If the task is limited to this question the cost analyst can select a format and comparable data that will provide a reasonably accurate projection. If costs appear to be constant across multiple alternatives (e.g., the cost of government performed quality assurance), then the analyst will not have to delve into the actual cost in order to develop a higher level of confidence in its accuracy. The estimate may be 20%

---

[32] Should-cost analyses and Life Cycle Cost Estimates (LCCE) are DoD prescribed documents.

too high or 15% too low but, since the same number is used for all the alternatives, it doesn't matter for this effort.[33] This rationale allows the cost analyst to devote time and expertise to the primary task of determining the *relative* cost of each alternative.

 If the cost analyst only has to answer the question as to the relative cost of each alternative, he/she will have much greater latitude in developing a reasonably accurate cost analysis in the difficult environment of incompatible cost accounting systems

Multiple Purposes for Cost Evaluations

If the BCA cost section is required to capture all costs for budget preparation, the cost evaluation task is seriously complicated. Different formats and data will be required. For example, the cost analyst may estimate and impute the value of office space, custodial services, and utilities for the BCA; however, these expenses are not paid by the government agency submitting a budget request.

A second argument for preparing a cost estimate tailored for the BCA question is that this decision frequently makes cost data collection easier. Government personnel are wary of providing cost estimates, particularly when efficiencies are being pursued. This comes from their experience of having their annual budgets reduced by the amount of savings they strive to achieve. The natural consequence is a reluctance to be honest about planned cost improvements. If it is clear to everyone that the BCA cost estimate does not cover all the costs and is not being prepared for the purpose of justifying budget requests, it is often easier to solicit the applicable cost data.

 Government personnel have learned to be evasive about projected cost efficiencies because the result may be reduced budgets. Contractor personnel have learned to underestimate costs because it facilitates getting the business and the actual contracted costs will be determined later. The result is the task of preparing BCA cost estimates requires an analyst who understands the costs, is imaginative in how to create comparable cost categories, and has the persuasion and tenacity of a good detective.

---

[33] Another example is that the cost analyst may be able to determine, with a reasonable level of confidence that the cost of transportation under alternative # 4 will be 12% higher than that of alternative # 1.   The analyst has little confidence that all the transportation costs are included in the estimate for alternative # 1 but, since the task is to find the relative cost of each alternative, he/she doesn't have to spend resources to thoroughly document the as-is costs (i.e., alternative # 1).

Cost Data Compatibility

The time period used for the cost analysis should be the same one that was identified at the *project definition* presentation for all facets of the BCA. Developing the cost section of the study typically requires a great many assumptions, due to data incompatibility. One example is labor cost. Commercial firms provide fully loaded labor rates, as shown below:

$39.06	Labor Cost ($75,000 salary ÷ 1,920 hours a year)
$12.50	Direct benefit costs (e.g., matching FICA, health care premiums, 401(k) matching)
$31.06	Overhead[34] (e.g., building space, office furniture, I/T, direct supervision)
$ 9.53	General & Administrative (e.g., corporate accounting, HR, contract management)
$ 5.77	Profit ("fee")
$97.92	Contract bill rate

The means of allocating labor cost is similar to what one encounters when taking a car in for service. The service garage uses a flat hourly rate to cover the cost of the mechanic's salary and benefits, as well as a portion of the facility, tooling, accounting, building, property taxes, and other expenses. This format is handy for the BCA cost analyst as it captures all the cost associated with the effort. The challenge is when the analyst attempts to compare this to a comparable government employee, as shown below:

$42.61	Labor Cost ($75,000 salary ÷ 1,760 hours a year[35]
$19.18	Direct benefit costs (e.g., retirement benefits, health insurance)
Unknown	Overhead (e.g., building space, utilities, telecommunications, direct supervision)
Unknown	General & Administrative (e.g., accounting systems, OMB[36], security, HR)
$ - 0 -	Profit
Unknown	Total hourly labor cost

These two examples illustrate the challenges of collecting and comparing costs. There are myriad costs that the government office or agency does not pay. These likely include building maintenance and repair, custodial services, grounds maintenance, security, training, legal fees, telecommunications, depreciation,[37] contract administration, payroll services, and others. There are also expenses that the government simply doesn't incur. Examples include property and vehicle insurance, industry association membership dues, accounting audits, stock related

---

[34] These accounting categories are defined and prescribed (i.e., what is to be included) by the federal government.
[35] Government employees typically receive more vacation days and more training days a year resulting in the lower figure for annual work hours)
[36] Office of Management & Budget
[37] When the government divides costs into the categories of "recurring" and "non-recurring" this is an implicit recognition of the effects of depreciation. However, the government cost accounting system does not collect nor account for depreciation of buildings, equipment, vehicles, etc.

expenses, and others. Other revenue and expense issues such as cash flow projections, that are so important to commercial firms, have little or no applicability to the government,[38] while commercial measures such as ROI have little applicability in the government.[39]

The BCA cost analyst(s) have a major challenge in the development of comparable data and metrics for commercial and government operations.

Cost Sub-categories

The government typically has policy and cost analyses guidance and manuals. Experienced government cost analysts generally have the expertise to develop a structure to capture the costs for a comparison. While the following list of cost categories is certainly not intended to be comprehensive, it is offered as a sampling of the considerations that might be included in the cost section of a BCA. Some of these data elements are not expressly collected and will have to be imputed:

- Acquisition costs (e.g., research, source selection boards, contracting)
- Facility and equipment upgrades
- Personnel training and qualifications
- Information technology
- Depreciation
- Management time and attention
- Travel
- Inherited assets
- Residual (salvage) value
- Military personnel
- Operating and support cost (e.g., tooling, database repositories, safety redesigns)
- Investment costs (e.g., military construction, initial spares, SCM[40] software, R&D)
- Auditing and other quality assurance efforts
- Security

Government cost analysts typically have extensive guidance and experience with this sort of analysis (e.g., policy guidance, cost manuals). Consequently, detailed instruction in this text is not provided as it would be duplicative or moot.

---

[38] Commercial BCAs texts will also address issues such as whether the calculations should be before-tax or after-tax. These are but some of the reasons for this book; that is, to provide BCA how-to guidance as it applies to federal agencies.
[39] For public agencies, a cost-benefit analysis in performed rather than a ROI calculation.
[40] Supply Chain Management

Standard financial criteria to evaluate expenses over several years also work well for government applications. Internal Rate of Return (IRR) and Net Present Value (NPV) are preferable to the payback period because the time periods are typically longer for operations evaluated with a BCA and these measures adjust for the time value of money.

Cost Assumptions

Like other sections of the BCA, the cost portion should be unique to the particular questions being addressed. This tailoring and the challenges of comparing cost data between commercial and government operations results in multiple assumptions. These assumptions should be explicit and included in the BCA, either in footnotes and/or appendices. The objective is not to get 100% agreement on every aspect of the cost methodology, but, rather, to provide clear and explicit information regarding the underlying assumptions.

Sunk costs (previously expended) should not be considered in any of the alternatives.

Forecasting Costs

Dealing with forecasting uncertainty over long periods (e.g., decades) is always a challenge. There are some good financial tools available for this. One of the most widely used is the Monte Carlo analysis which runs the projections several times under varying scenarios. This, and other tools used in commercial applications (notably investments), can be applied to government applications. Before using one of these financial tools the cost analyst should check with the government agency to determine if they have a list of approved financial methods for dealing with uncertainty over long periods. When feasible, the cost analyst should include measures of confidence for projections stemming from sampling.[41]

Despite the difference with respect to data availability, it is essential that the cost analysis be consistent in the manner in which costs are collected and assessed across each of the alternatives.

---

[41] The sampling size determines the level of confidence achieved, e.g., an 80% confidence coefficient. Oftentimes, this level of calculation is not required. As an example, one may provide cost comparison data on 12 overhaul components and explain why these 12 reflect the total components or that these 12 were selected because they're the only ones for which comparable data was available. Then provide the decision maker with a non-calculated estimate of how confident the analyst is in the forecast accuracy of the cost comparisons.

Converting Findings to a Cost Scorecard

An issue arises with respect to converting the findings of the cost section to scores that are compatible with the rest of the BCA. An example is depicted below.

	Alternative # 1	Alternative # 2	Alternative # 3	Alternative # 4
Technical (30%)	20.6	16.0	21.6	23.1
Operational (40%)	20.1	23.8	27.2	27.9
Risk (10%)	6.4	8.5	7.9	5.3
Cost (20%)	$19,281,349	$23,568,455	$26,588,024	$20,851,361

The difficulty in the previous example is that there does not exist a straight-forward formula to convert these financial projections to scores. Assuming that the most this operation should cost is $30 million, a cost of $30 million will receive a score of zero. The best possible outcome would be no cost, which would result in a score of 100 (or 20 in this example[42]). Using a linear relationship results in the following scores.

	Alternative # 1	Alternative # 2	Alternative # 3	Alternative # 4
Technical (30%)	20.6	16.0	21.6	23.1
Operational (40%)	20.1	23.8	27.2	27.9
Risk (10%)	6.4	8.5	7.9	5.3
Cost (20%)	7.1	4.3	2.3	6.1
	54.2	52.6	59.0	62.4

The problem with this approach is obvious in that the linear score ratios do not agree with the relative cost ratio. The highest cost (alternative # 3) is 38% higher than the lowest cost (alternative # 1). However, this scoring results in a 68% difference between alternative #1 and alternative #3. Using these parameters (linear scale between 0 and $30 million) magnifies the cost differences beyond what they should be.

Be careful not to introduce unintentional (or intentional!) bias in the manner in which cost projections are converted to BCA scores.

---

[42] Since, in this example, cost accounts for 20% of the total possible points (i.e., the pre-determined relative weighting) then the most points that can be assigned are 20.

Some judgment is required in developing the scoring conversion scale. That is, a range of $18 million to $28 million could be justified, resulting in the following scores.

	Alternative # 1	Alternative # 2	Alternative # 3	Alternative # 4
Technical (30%)	20.6	16.0	21.6	23.1
Operational (40%)	20.1	23.8	27.2	27.9
Risk (10%)	6.4	8.5	7.9	5.3
Cost (20%)	17.4	8.9	2.8	14.3
	64.5	56.2	59.5	70.6

By further narrowing the range, the scoring results still do not reflect the relativity of the cost estimates. While the actual cost difference is 38%, the scoring delta is magnified to 84%. Although the conversion of dollar figures to BCA scores requires some judgment and entails some latitude, the method used is far from arbitrary. The end objective of the study is to provide the decision maker with a scoring means which is in accordance with the decision criterion (relative weights) that was selected at the *project definition* presentation. Great effort needs to be taken to avoid any scoring method that skews the results.

A better solution would be to take the same approach but alter the high and low cost ranges. This time, assume that an exceptionally efficient operation might be able to perform the operation at a cost of $15 million and a terribly inefficient operation would cost $40 million. Use the same linear conversion method, but this time the scale will be 20 points at $15 million and zero points at $40 million. This scoring result follows.

	Alternative # 1	Alternative # 2	Alternative # 3	Alternative # 4
Technical (30%)	20.6	16.0	21.6	23.1
Operational (40%)	20.1	23.8	27.2	27.9
Risk (10%)	6.4	8.5	7.9	5.3
Cost (20%)	16.6	13.2	10.7	15.3
	65.0	59.1	62.4	71.7

As opposed to the previous two examples, this conversion is much better scaled to provide the decision maker with information in accordance to the decision criterion identified at the *project definition* presentation. The highest cost (alternative # 3) is 38% higher than the lowest cost (alternative # 1) and the delta between the scores is a comparable 35%. This separation between the financial scores also makes intuitive sense. It is not as important how high or low the scores are, but rather that the scores reflect the relativity of the cost estimates.

The conversion of projections from dollar figures to scores requires judgment but it is far from arbitrary. Every effort needs to be taken to avoid a method that skews the cost impact.

Sensitivity Analysis

The purpose of a sensitivity analysis is to determine the cost impact of altering some of the study assumptions. For example, one of the assumptions related to the capacity of the U.S. national airspace may be linear projections of past daily flights to develop projected usage. Over the course of the *primary research* phase the BCA team may learn of policy discussions related to the use of unmanned aircraft in the U.S. civil airspace. Either as a result of their own findings or as a consequence of direction from the study sponsor, the cost analyst may run cost projections under a different scenario, e.g., with a 5% increase in usage due to the introduction of unmanned aircraft. How does this change to one of the assumptions alter the scoring of each alternative?

Using the same example, the team may be asked to assess a scenario in which the next generation of air traffic control technology permits a 30% increase to the en route volume of aircraft. If the spreadsheets have been constructed in a conscientious and deliberate manner, these should be relatively easy answers to provide.

The purpose of sensitivity analysis is to run what-if scenarios when one of the original assumptions changes or when there are subsequent inquiries as to the whether a major change would alter the selected alternative.

Occasionally, requests for such what-if scenarios require scoring revisions in the non-cost categories but this is the exception.[43] Also, requests for such what-if scenarios should be discouraged if they entail entirely new, and previously not discussed, alternatives. Those who suggest such answers should be reminded that this was the point of the *project definition* presentation, that is, to ensure that all understood what was going to be analyzed *before* the primary research phase commenced.

Ancillary Findings

During the course of the study, the team will encounter all manner of information that is related to the operation but not directly relevant to the BCA. The ancillary findings section lists findings that are separate from the analysis but may be of value to the decision maker.

---

[43] If the impact of altering an assumption only affects cost (which is typically the case) then, of course, only the cost score has the potential to change. If the cost scores are close and/or cost accounts for less than 30% of the total score for each alternative, it is uncommon for these what-if scenarios to alter the alternative with the highest score.

Effective managers want to hear the perspective of outside observers who have conducted multiple BCAs and spent considerable time inside their operation. The documentation and wording of the ancillary findings requires a high level of management sensitivity and awareness to avoid documenting shortcomings of the very client who hired them. However, providing useful information when it is available is also important. If the study results will be reviewed by higher level headquarters or other agencies, it may be preferable to provide the ancillary findings in a stand-alone document separate from the BCA.[44]

The following list shows examples of the type of ancillary findings that might be provided in the conduct of a BCA:

- Organizational structure
- Coordination with other government offices and agencies
- Targeted training for key individuals
- Identification (and potential remedies) of bottlenecks
- Vulnerabilities (e.g., accounting practices likely to be challenged during an audit)
- Observations regarding employee morale
- Security awareness
- Processes which may be considered for re-engineering
- Attitudes or practices that may impede *best value* competitive selections
- The need for updated and/or improved policies and/or procedures
- Best practices to consider for application to another aspect of the organization

In some BCAs, the ancillary findings are considered the most valuable information provided. Oftentimes these lead to other improvements in the organization.

Emerging Results Presentation

The culmination of the *primary research* phase is the *emerging results* presentation. The purpose of the *emerging results* presentation is twofold. First, by apprising the study sponsor and advisory council (if applicable) of the preliminary findings, the BCA team can learn of any aspect of their research which may be lacking. These experienced managers may note aspects of the research that don't appear to make sense. It is possible that initial findings may not consider all the germane factors necessary to reach a conclusion, or it may be that greater detail and/or data accuracy will be requested to support a finding. By holding an *emerging results* presentation weeks before the final report is due, the BCA team is afforded the opportunity to conduct additional, unplanned research and still meet the original study deadline.

---

[44] Depending on the relationship that has developed between the BCA team leader and the study sponsor, it may also be appropriate for him/her to relay a particular observation via verbal means only.

By scheduling the *emerging results* presentation weeks before the final report is due, the analysts are afforded the opportunity to conduct additional, unplanned research on particular topic areas if necessary.

The second reason to schedule an *emerging results* presentation is to provide key leaders with advance notice of findings and/or recommendations that may be controversial. For example, if the clear and distinct recommendation is an alternative that will be disruptive to the organization and will likely result in sensitivity to perceived criticism, it is certainly preferable for the managers to know this in advance of the final report. This additional time allows the manager to inform senior executives and take steps to mitigate a negative reaction.

Additionally, if the majority of the scores are available, they should be presented at the *emerging results* presentation. This gives credibility to the research and findings. Also, many times it is apparent that, even though some gaps remain, the outcome is clear (i.e., which alternative(s) are *not* going to be recommended). If there is disagreement over a particular score it will often be evident that it doesn't matter. That is, the overall relative weighting of the score in question is such that spending additional resources to reevaluate this area will serve no purpose.

Since these are emerging findings, it is appropriate to have blank spaces in the overall scorecard where some data collection and analysis are not yet complete.

Ancillary findings are not generally addressed at the *emerging results* presentation. Typically, there are a great deal of the primary findings to address and this, of course, takes priority. Also, the ancillary findings are frequently not yet assembled by the BCA team. Finally, the ancillary findings are just that. They aren't central to the study and normally don't warrant time on the agenda at this crucial presentation. However, these are just guidelines related to convenience and timing. If the BCA team leader and/or study sponsor want to address some or all of the ancillary findings at this forum, there are no compelling reasons to avoid doing so.

As a general rule, the ancillary findings are not addressed at the emerging results presentation. There are too many other essential discussion points and the BCA team leader will not want to divert attention to these secondary items.

Be sure to schedule adequate time for the *emerging results* presentation. This presentation gives the decision maker and affected managers their first opportunity to review the study results and consider the consequences. The study team leader has a strong preference to have substantive issues addressed at this forum, rather than at the final BCA presentation. Depending on the size and complexity of the BCA, substantial data and presentations may be provided by each of the study analysts.

The attendee list at the *emerging results* presentation should be limited; otherwise, one risks spawning disruptive rumors stemming from incomplete analyses.

Chapter 7: Final Research Phase

Executive Summary

Depending on the size and complexity of the BCA, the *final research* phase ranges from several weeks to several months. The *final results* presentation should be comprehensive and yet not include substantial surprises. Findings and recommendations are typically different chapters or sub-sections of the final report. Recommendations should include general milestones and activities but not detailed implementation planning. The alternative selected by the BCA team is normally the one that receives the highest score but not always so. The study contains important information that the study sponsor will consider although other information may also be available and the study sponsor may not select the alternative recommended by the analysts. It is essential that the final written report be complete enough to provide important information for those who will implement the changes and for managers who are later assigned to the operations, as well as provide a documented source of decisions for subsequent reviews.

Introduction

The *final research* phase commences after the completion of the *emerging results* presentation and ends with delivery of the *final report*. Depending on the size and complexity of the BCA, this period can range from two weeks to two month. Since the emerging results were just that, the study analysts will typically have additional research and documentation planned. Also, as described in the previous chapter, the *emerging results* presentation may result in additional, unplanned research. At this point the BCA team leader will need to carefully manage the remaining effort to match the time available.

As a general statement, the content writing must be completed no later than a week to ten days prior to the final deadline. The last week of the study will be taken by proofreading, grammar and punctuation corrections, printing, and binding. During this final week the team members can prepare final contractual documents[45] and write after-action reports. This means the final report presentation should be scheduled for a date ten to fourteen days prior to the final BCA deadline. This timing allows the analysts to include any minor content or wording changes that are the result of the *final BCA* presentation.

> Changes to the final report that result from the final BCA presentation should be minor in nature. Substantive changes should have been identified at the emerging results presentation.

---

[45] Typically referred to as Contract Data Requirements List (CDRL) documents.

Final Results Presentation

The BCA final results presentation should be methodical and comprehensive. If the *emerging results* presentation was conducted well, this presentation and ensuing discussions may not take as much time. There should not be any major surprises at this point, i.e., findings or recommendations that vary substantially from those discussed at the *emerging results* presentation.

The final BCA presentation should not include any substantial surprises.

New information provided at this point typically includes the ancillary findings.[46] These often result in significant discussion. Hence, adequate time should be planned on the agenda. The *final research* phase also provides enough time for the study analysts to develop recommendations. While a large study may include ten to twenty findings (separately identified), this may result in three to six recommended actions. This is because the implementation of a recommendation will often address multiple findings. Recommendations should be specific enough to provide value to the study sponsor, but not be so detailed as to assume the duties of managers whose responsibility it is to plan and execute changes. For example, broad schedules and major events sequentially identified should be provided.[47] However, detailed implementation planning should be conducted by those who will have the eventual responsibility for the success of the operation.

Providing broad schedules of events in the recommendations section are appropriate; providing detailed planning is not. This is the prerogative and responsibility of the government employees who are responsible for the implementation and eventual success of the operation.

Recommendations should also include key success criterion and *exit ramps*. An example follows: "If accurate, complete, and timely databases are not developed and available at the desktop within six months, this alternative should be re-evaluated and consideration given to canceling the change and reverting to alternative # 1."

---

[46] The exception to this is when some or all the ancillary findings are sensitive and provided to the study sponsor in a separate document.

[47] While these broad events and milestones might be provided on a Gantt schedule, the analysts should be careful to not provide specific dates and predecessor activities. These are the prerogative and responsibility of the government personnel who will have implementation responsibility.

The recommendation section should generally include key progress criterion and exit ramps. That is, if the selected alternative is not working out, then what action should be taken and when.

Final Scoring

One aspect of BCAs that is always intriguing is the variance between the total scores of each alternative. Two examples are provided below.

	Relative Weight	Alternative #1		Alternative #2		Alternative #3		Alternative #4		Alternative #5	
		Raw Score	Weighted Score	Raw Score	Weighted Score	Raw Score	Weighted Score	Raw Score	Weighted Score	Raw Score	Weighted Score
Operational	50%										
Subfactor A (20% of "Operational")		8	8.00	5	5.00	6	6.00	5	5.00	9	9.00
Subfactor B (30% of Operational")		9	13.50	8	13.50	6	13.50	8	13.50	8	13.50
Subfactor C (10% of Operational")		7	3.50	2	1.00	4	2.00	7	3.50	7	3.50
Subfactor D (25% of Operational")		7	8.75	3	3.75	7	8.75	7	8.75	7	8.75
Subfactor E (15% of Operational")		8	6.0	5	3.75	8	6.00	8	6.00	8	6.00
Operational Subtotal =			39.75		27.00		36.25		36.75		40.75
Risk	15%	8	12.00	6	9.00	9	13.50	8	12.00	8	12.00
Cost	35%	9	31.50	5.5	19.25	8.6	30.10	8.8	30.80	9.1	31.85
Final Score	100%		83.3%		55.3%		79.9%		79.6%		84.6%

In the previous instance there is one poorly scoring alternative, two comparable choices in the mid range, and two alternatives which have close scores indicating the optimal solution. Two important points should be raised for a scoring outcome such as this. First, alternatives # 1 and # 5 are essentially equivalent. These two scores are separated by 1.3 points. It is highly unlikely that the BCA estimate, with all of the requirements to convert subjective evaluations to objective scores, is so accurate that the analysts will want to unequivocally state that alternative # 5 is superior to alternative # 1. The fact is that these scores are most likely to be well within the margin of error of the study. The second point is that if alternative # 1 is the status quo,[48] then the obvious recommendation is that no change occurs.[49] This is because two alternatives are, for all practical purposes, equivalent. Without the expectation of appreciable improvement, one should not embark on a disruptive change.

---

[48] While there is no reason to number the alternatives in any particular sequence, by convention, the status quo is identified as alternative # 1.

[49] One should not conclude from an outcome such as this, that the BCA was not necessary. First of all, it confirmed that the current operation is the optimal one. This, in itself, is valuable information. Secondly, the ancillary findings alone may result in improvements that justified the study cost and effort.

	Relative Weight	Alternative #1		Alternative #2		Alternative #3		Alternative #4		Alternative #5	
		Raw Score	Weighted Score	Raw Score	Weighted Score	Raw Score	Weighted Score	Raw Score	Weighted Score	Raw Score	Weighted Score
Operational	50%										
Subfactor A (20% of "Operational")		7	7.00	8	8.00	10	10.00	9	9.00	9	9.00
Subfactor B (30% of Operational")		6	9.00	8	9.00	8	9.00	8	9.00	8	9.00
Subfactor C (10% of Operational")		6	3.00	7	3.50	7	3.50	7	3.50	10	5.00
Subfactor D (25% of Operational")		7	8.75	6	7.50	10	12.50	7	8.75	9	11.25
Subfactor E (15% of Operational")		8	6.00	10	7.50	8	6.00	9	6.75	8	6.00
Operational Subtotal =			33.75		35.50		41.00		37.00		40.25
Risk	15%	7	10.50	9	13.50	9	13.50	7	10.50	8	12.00
Cost		8	28.00	7.8	27.30	9.4	32.90	7.8	27.30	6.6	23.10
Final Score	100%		72.3%		76.3%		87.4%		74.8%		75.4%

In the previous example, one clear and distinct superior solution exists. The practical aspect of this outcome is less discussion regarding the scoring. When the completed scorecards are provided, challenging any single score will have no effect on the final recommendation (e.g., this particular logistics sub-category should be a 4 rather than a 3).

Recommended Alternative

The BCA team typically recommends the highest scoring alternative. However, this is not always the case. When two or three alternatives have similar scores, the superior solution is not evident. The study analysts may consider other factors they have learned during the assessment to develop and explain their recommendation. These may include subjective considerations such as facilities, the enthusiasm and obvious expertise of personnel, a penchant for constant improvement, and/or how disruptive a change will be compared to the expected gain. Of course, whatever the final recommendation is, it needs to be accompanied by the objective and subjective rationale for its selection.

Alternative Selection

The BCA team needs to keep in mind that they are researching and developing *recommendations* for the study sponsor. Sometimes the analysts have so much invested in the BCA that they begin to think they are in a position to decide the optimal solution. This is not the case! The study analysts are temporary consultants on a particular topic. This is true even when the team consists of all government personnel. The responsibility for the operation remains with the study sponsor. It is the responsibility of the study sponsor, alone, to make the final decision as to which alternative to select. It is the study sponsor's prerogative to decide how much weight to give the BCA in the final decision. The manager is experienced and undoubtedly has explicit information, knowledge, and other factors to consider in deciding the optimal solution. The study analysts need to be diligent and conscientious but, at the same time, keep in mind that they have neither the authority nor the responsibility to make this decision. This is easier to accept if the study sponsor selects an alternative which scores close to the highest scoring one. Regardless of the outcome selected, the analysts need to understand their role.

The final decision as to which alternative to select remains solely with the responsible government manager.

Documentation

There is an unfortunate trend away from comprehensive documentation of substantive research, findings, and recommendations. In some cases, the study sponsor and/or advisory council will be satisfied with PowerPoint charts presented at the *final report* presentation. Key decision makers may not even read the complete written report. This does not negate the need for one. Most often the operation being assessed is substantial in nature. The managerial attention and funds needed to implement the change are large. The time required is often years as changes occur in organizational structure, new leadership, technology, and other areas. New leaders or external reviews need to have access to the information that was known and considered relevant to the decision that was made. PowerPoint bullet points are incapable of capturing research and supporting rationale. One of the recurring lessons learned is that by failing to carefully document the as-is model, to include cost, "…managers won't have baseline information which is needed to evaluate future outcomes and determine whether they achieved benefits with their strategy."[50] A comprehensive written report is essential.

---

[50] U.S. Army Audit Agency audit report A-2007-0072-ALM dated 9 February 2007: "Army's Process and Controls for Effectively Implementing Performance-Based Logistics", page 9.

Without thorough documentation, one will be unable to determine if the selected strategy worked or know what adjustments will lead to further improvements.

Chapter 8: Implementation

Executive Summary

In some instances, the completion of the study will result in the disbanding of the BCA team. In other cases, it will be advantageous to retain some of the analysts for the subsequent implementation. When this is done, a separate contract or contract option is preferable. However, when the retention of particular experienced contractors is desired, care needs to be taken to ensure there is not a gap between the two contract efforts. A well-conducted BCA is a particularly effective tool for the manager who is pursuing improvement.

Completing the Study

If the BCA has been properly structured, the primary manager(s), who will be directly affected by the recommended changes, participated in determining what to assess (the *project definition* presentation), reviewed interim progress, was involved in the discussion of preliminary findings (the *emerging findings* presentation), and was an active participant in the study conclusions (the *final results* presentation). Also, the final report has thoroughly documented the as-is model, the analyses which led to the recommended actions, and moderately detailed implementation recommendations. In many instances, the BCA team has completed its job and can be disbanded at this point.

The implementation of the changes necessary to convert from the current operation to the selected alternative can range from relatively simple to difficult transitions. Nevertheless, the change-management skills and tools associated with this implementation typically reside within the government office or agency. The timetable selected for each aspect of the implementation, the funding, contracting actions, coordination, and personnel assignments are all the responsibility of the manager. Furthermore, these are inherently government functions and little of this activity can be contracted out to consultants.

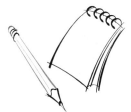

Many of the implementation tasks are inherently government functions.

Implementation

A general recommendation is that implementation tasks should be performed by those who have responsibility over the existing and new operation. These employees are the ones who have the greatest detailed knowledge and are the ones who will need to develop the specific steps and make the inevitable adjustments associated with a successful change effort.

The preponderance of the implementation tasks needs to be performed by those who will have the long term responsibility for the operation.

Occasionally the government manager will want to retain some or all of the BCA analysts to assist in the implementation. If the change effort is large or the operation is being transitioned to one that is unfamiliar to the current government personnel (e.g., a commercial practice), then the BCA analysts are often those most familiar with both the as-is and the to-be operation. If the option is available the manager may retain some of these personnel as advisors to the government personnel who will implement the changes. Of course, depending on the organization and working relationships, these advisors can perform more or less of the required tasks. [51]

In some cases, the BCA was initially performed for the sole purpose of identifying the methods by which a change can occur. The DoD Performance Based Logistics (PBL) initiatives are a case in point. PBL is a practice by where the government alters their practice of contracting for items (e.g., the purchase of 400 tires to be warehoused) to contracting for performance (e.g., 95% of tire orders will be filled within 24 hours). Prior to the implementation of a PBL solution, DoD policy appropriately requires a BCA. In these instances the BCA is the first of a three-step process.[52]

In these cases, the manager may develop a plan to use the same personnel throughout the entire change process. The rationale is that during the conduct of the BCA these analysts have become the most knowledgeable personnel with respect to the current operation, the newly selected operation, and what is required to transition from one to the other. In this example, it may be that only the team leader, the logistician, and the junior planner continue with the PBL implementation effort and the other members of the BCA team (e.g., the cost analysts) be moved to other projects at the completion of the BCA.

The ideal team members for the BCA will not necessarily be the same ones for the subsequent implementation phase.

---

[51] Change management activities that can be performed by contractor personnel include preparation and staffing of the master plan, the preparation of funding request documents and supporting rationale, Gantt schedules, communication with affected personnel and offices, progress tracking (e.g., Earned Value Management System), facility layouts, transportation, and other related tasks.

[52] The analyses is performed (the BCA); then the implantation occurs (a performance based contract or agreement); and then confirmation of desired outcomes and modifications, as necessary, take place.

Regardless of whether the original intent is a BCA as a stand-alone study or whether it is part of a larger change endeavor, the BCA should be planned (and/or contracted) as a distinct effort. Frequently, the personnel skills needed for the BCA will differ from the ideal team assembled for the subsequent implementation phase. Also, it helps everyone track progress and commitment to deadlines if the BCA has a predetermined lifespan. The nature of all research is that more detail can be assembled and analyzed. Long running BCAs allow for more diversions, are more likely to have turnover in the personnel, and oftentimes will be updating previous findings with more current organization, policies, technology, or other changes which occur during the course of the study.

When contracting for BCA services, contract separately for the study itself and any subsequent support, in part, because the type of work is different. Also, the implementation tasks will not be known until the BCA reaches the *emerging results* presentation at the earliest. Consequently, the appropriate assistance may not be known when the initial contract for the study is signed. Another consideration is that, until the BCA is well underway, the government will not have experience with the analysts and know whether they want to retain them for subsequent assistance. Still another important consideration is maintaining objectivity. When the analysts view alternatives, human tendency is to look more favorably on the people and institutions already known. Part of this is comfort in remaining with those who one knows and part of it is compassion towards those who might be adversely impacted by a finding. These sentiments (and influences) are contrary to the objectives of the BCA.

Even when the eventual plan is to use the BCA analysts for implementation, these subsequent tasks should be a separate contract or an option to the first one.

The obvious challenge with this approach is that it risks the loss of key personnel if there is a gap between the BCA and the subsequent implementation. Sometimes the government manager will take a few weeks or months to get approval for the planned implementation and then another few weeks will be required for the contracting actions. When this occurs the analysts that performed the study will likely not be available.[53] If anticipating the use of some of the non-government BCA analysts for subsequent work, the government manager needs to be proactive. By the middle of the BCA, the study sponsor should have a good sense of whether these individuals will be needed. If so, the government manager needs to have the funding identified and other preliminary contracting actions complete by the time of the *emerging results* presentation. Then, if the decision is made to use some, or all, of the study analysts, the follow-on contract can be in place before the BCA contract ends.

---

[53] Nationwide, there are very few analysts who have experience with conducting multiple government BCAs which are properly structured, have conclusions and recommendations supported by facts, are comprehensive enough to be audited, and thorough enough to be useful in later years to determine success.

Top notch, experienced BCA analysts are hard to come by. If there's a gap between the end of the BCA and a subsequent desire to use these personnel, it's unlikely that they'll be available.

Summary

A structured and well conducted BCA is a valuable and effective tool for the manager who is striving to pursue improvement. Whether the study is required or conducted at the initiative of the manager, it needs to be executed well. Like all major endeavors that have the potential for substantive change, this one requires the active participation of the manager. An effective BCA should have the following characteristics:

- Experienced and capable analysts without a bias towards the outcome
- Analysts with the skills for this particular study
- Three distinct phases
- Scope, assumptions, alternatives, and decision criteria tailored to the particular operation being assessed
- Too many alternatives initially are preferable than too few
- Comprehensive documentation of the as-is model (including costs) so that subsequent evaluations can be determined as to the effectiveness of the change
- Resources spent should be commensurate with the expected gains from the change
- Reasonable time limits to ensure the study is complete in a timely manner and to the appropriate depth of analysis
- Adequate controversy is probably a sign for substantive change
- Relevant parties and issues present at the beginning and the end
- No substantial surprises in the final presentation
- All sources are referenced
- An exit strategy is included, i.e., if projected improvements are not achieved
- The analysis was conducted with the taxpayer in mind, i.e., to include *all* the projected benefits compared to *all* the costs
- All the factors important to the decision, not just the ones which have readily available, objective measures
- The BCA results are data available to the decision maker.
- Supporting empirical data tailored to the scope and consistent across the alternatives
- Cost projections formatted such that, in subsequent years, it will be possible to determine whether the cost improvements (if planned) have been achieved
- Ancillary findings included
- Sufficient detail to commence implementation planning

For all the government managers who pursue improvement, it is my sincere hope that this text will be of value.

Ron Klein
Huntsville, AL
January, 2008

————————

As stated in the introduction, this book was written to address the void in texts related to practical, hands-on advice as to how to conduct Business Case Analyses in the public sector. Comments regarding this attempt are solicited. rklein@belzon.com

Appendices

A. Helpful BCA practices
B. Common characteristics to include in the cost section of DoD BCAs
C. Converting cost estimates to a score
D. Other Reference Sources
E. Acronyms

Appendix A: Helpful BCA Practices

1. When interviewing sources, attempt to have as many conversations as needed in any order that personnel are available. Do not plan on sequential interviews or delay progress because someone is unavailable.

2. Promotions, retirements, and transfers occur. The longer the BCA, the more personnel changes (e.g., sources cited). Clear documentation and understanding cannot only help the analyst in continuing to move forward, but can also assist incoming personnel.

3. If it becomes obvious the current source will have to seek other sources, it is a good practice for the analyst to conduct this research and gather data directly from the secondary source. This practice aids the source, minimizes communication filters, and can add to documentation to support objectivity.

4. Know what you know. Know what you don't know.

5. Sometimes the data doesn't exist. Know when to stop looking.

6. Sometimes the data discovery process is too expensive and/or time consuming. It may not be worth it.

7. Understand and document the difference between facts and valid personnel assessments.

8. Avoid including opinions when data exists (i.e., as a shortcut to data collection).

9. Gather information from individual sources and confirm the accuracy of that information with the source. If you share the source information with individuals, they generally will analyze their position and attempt to make changes to highlight strengths and mitigate weaknesses. This results in a time consuming effort that is defensive in nature and inappropriately assists the naysayer. It is better to share the emerging results with the designated study sponsor or advisory board and, when the time is appropriate, let them send it to the appropriate senior mangers.

10. Develop a framework for the research. For example, have folders for funding, equipment flow, data flow, material, decision process, quality control, and administration.

11. Clearly defined categories of data and scope limit chasing rabbits. A properly managed timeline also helps, as the work expands to fill the time available.

12. Subject matter experts tend to stray out of their area of expertise. Be sure to understand where fact becomes opinion and help keep people in their lane.

13. Sometimes the best answer is complex, entails conflict, and is difficult to capture. If the organization and supporting members get frustrated, there is a tendency to move toward an easy answer for the illusion of progress. Avoid the temptation of the consensus rather than the good research, analyses, and documentation.

14. Document the sources for all facts and statements. A footnote with the person's name, organization, and date will often suffice.

15. Beware those who quote policy to avoid change. Waivers to policy are the prerogative of senior leaders.

16. Sometimes the optimal solution is as simple as identifying a single point of responsibility and authority over the *entire* operation.

17. Cultural attitudes are difficult to measure and more difficult to alter. Not paying adequate attention to underlying cultural preferences and beliefs nearly always makes the task much more difficult.

18. Keep your eye on the ball. Nearly everyone wants to be better at what they do. Keep reminding participants that this is what the BCA is, that is, it is an analysis to identify the best means to perform the mission.

19. Tension exists between constantly keeping everyone informed and getting the research and findings done on time.

20. Be committed to the analyses but, at the same time, don't get too emotionally invested in the outcome. The BCA is essential information to a decision maker, but many times the optimal solution is not necessarily the highest scoring alternative.

Appendix B: Common Characteristics to Include in the Cost Section of DoD BCAs[54]

1. Base Year is the year the study occurs.

2. Latest indices from OSD per reference, except as amended below; exceptions must be annotated in the BCA.

3. Latest discount rates from the OMB per Appendix C of reference, except as amended below; exceptions must be annotated in the BCA.

4. The BCA must identify budgetable (hard) savings benefits that can be measured, quantified, or placed under control.

5. Any cost avoidance (cost savings) in labor hours or dollars should be addressed as a separate line item.

6. No sunk costs (previously expended) are to be included in calculations or ROI analysis.

7. Labor rate costing per reference for military/civilians will be used, except as amended below; exceptions must be annotated in the BCA.

8. A total life cycle cost approach will be used across the relevant life cycle (remaining years of service for the supported item scope being analyzed).

9. All cost elements impacted by the PBL strategy shall be addressed.

10. Non-financial benefits will be considered and explained.

11. Sensitivity analysis will be included (usually expressed as ROI and/or breakeven analysis).

---

[54] Department of the Navy Guide for Developing Performance Based Logistics Business Case Analyses (P07-006), dated November 06, 2007

Appendix C: Converting Cost Estimates to a Score

There are two main objectives that need to be accomplished in the conversion process: (1) the lowest cost (most desirable) should receive the highest score and (2) scoring should reflect the relativity of the cost estimates. Applying a linear formula, if applied properly, to the cost estimates can generate a numerical score which accomplishes these two objectives. In the following scenario, the numbers are simplified to make the example and the reasoning behind the analysis clearer.

Scenario

- For this example the BCA has 3 alternatives. The cost estimate of each alternative is:
  - Alternative 1: $30 million
  - Alternative 2: $20 million
  - Alternative 3: $15 million
- The cost portion of the BCA is weighted as 25% of the total score.
- The lowest cost estimate is 50% lower than the highest. One of the primary objectives of the cost conversion is for the score to mirror the 50% difference between the low and high cost estimates.
    The cost difference is 50%, i.e., 50% of $30 million is $15 million.

Simple solution

A simple scoring rationale could be set up which would only address one issue; that is, giving the lowest cost the highest score. Say the lowest cost gets the highest score (100% of the total possible points or a score of 25 in this example) and the highest cost gets the lowest possible score (0); then, the difference between the low and high scores is 100%, which does not reflect the actual relationship between the estimated costs.

	Alt. #3	Alt. #1	Percentage
Cost	$15M	$30M	50%
Score	25	0	∞ %

The target ratio for both cost and scoring is 50%.

The problem with this simple conversion is that the ratio between costs and the ratio between the applied scores needs to be the same (or at least close). In this example, the actual cost difference is 50% and the applied score difference is infinite. Using this simple conversion will skew the scorecard results. The result will be too punitive for alternative # 1 and too generous for alternative # 3. This is reflected in the following calculations.

	High # Range	- Cost Estimate	/ Delta of the Range	* Weight	= Score
Alternative 1	30	30	15	25	0
Alternative 2	30	20	15	25	16.6
Alternative 3	30	15	15	25	25

Alternative 1: (30-30)/15*25=0
Alternative 2: (30-20)/15*25=16.6
Alternative 3: (30-15)/15*25=25

This scoring does not accurately reflect the relative difference between the cost estimates and will inadvertently alter your overall scoring outcome. A better method, explained below, is to develop a formula.

Develop a formula

A better method is to set up a possible range for the cost estimates, going above and below the high and low estimates. The next step is to apply a linear formula to convert the cost estimates to a score based on the set range. To convert the estimates to scores we used the following linear formula:

*(high # in range – cost estimate)/delta * the weight*

where

high # in range	=	The highest number of the set range.
cost estimate	=	The amount of each alternative's cost estimate.
delta	=	The difference between the highest number in the range and the lowest number in the range.
the weight	=	The weight given to the cost portion of the BCA.

In this formula, each alternative's cost estimate is subtracted from the high number established for the range. This inverts your cost estimates from high to low. That number is then divided by the delta of the range to give you a relative percentage. This percentage is multiplied by the weight given to the cost portion of the BCA to give a final numerical score.

In the previous example, the selected range is $15 million to $30 million. Consequently, the high number in range is $30 million. The cost estimate for alternative #1 is $30 million. In this example the range is from $15 million to $30 million. Consequently, the delta is $15 million. If cost accounts for 30% of the total BCA score then the weight is 30.

A key component to the success of this process is the establishment of the range of possible estimates. The range should be set below the lowest estimate and far enough above the highest to accurately reflect the inversion from high to low.

Example using the formula with a wider range

This example sets a more realistic range that will reflect the actual range of possible cost estimates. No program is ever going to cost zero dollars and the highest estimate, is just that, an estimate. Realistically, we could set the range from $10 million to $35 million, which is just above and just below the high and low estimates and the difference between the low and high in this range is $25 million. The following chart shows the scoring using this extended range. The lowest score now reflects the highest cost, and is 75% lower than the highest score and the lowest cost. This again does not reflect the actual relativity of the cost estimates.

	High # Range	- Cost Estimate	/ Delta of the Range	* Weight	= Score
Alternative 1	$35M	$30M	$25M	25	5
Alternative 2	$35M	$20M	$25M	25	15
Alternative 3	$35M	$15M	$25M	25	20

Alternative 1: (35-30)/25*25=5
Alternative 2: (35-20)/25*25=15
Alternative 3: (35-15)/25*25=20

	Alt. # 3	Alt. # 1	Percentage
Cost	$15M	$30M	50%
Score	20	5	75%

So, while this difference between the cost estimates and the scores are closer, greater accuracy can be achieved. This example is provided to illustrate the iterative process that is often required to develop an accurate conversion scale.

Example with appropriate range

Assume that an exceptionally poorly managed operation would cost as much as $45 million and, in ideal circumstances, the operation could cost as little as $10 million. This range of $10 million to $45 million results in scores that better reflect the actual cost estimate differences. The range is not necessarily the range of the possible cost estimates but the range that will let you accurately invert the estimates from low to high (the first step of the formula - high number of the range minus the cost estimates). The range may need to be adjusted so that the final scores reflect the actual relationship between the cost estimates.

	High # Range	- Cost Estimate	/ Delta of the Range	* Weight	= Score
Alternative 1	$45M	$30M	$35M	25	10.71
Alternative 2	$45M	$20M	$35M	25	17.85
Alternative 3	$45M	$15M	$35M	25	21.43

$$\text{Alternative 1:} \quad (45-30)/35*25=10.71$$
$$\text{Alternative 2:} \quad (45-20)/35*25=17.85$$
$$\text{Alternative 3:} \quad (45-15)/35*25=21.43$$

This conversion method has achieved the results we want. The lowest score is 50% lower than the highest. This is the same as the actual cost estimate difference. This scoring method will accurately reflect the relationship between the cost estimates ensuring that the cost score does not inadvertently alter the overall objectivity of the total scores.

	Alt. # 3	Alt. # 1	Percentage
Cost	$15M	$30M	50%
Score	21.43	10.71	50%

Again, the point of this exercise is to be able to provide the decision maker(s) with a single scorecard that is consistent with the evaluation criteria (and, in particular, the relative weightings) that he/she chose at the *project definition* presentation. This also allows for relatively easy sensitivity analyses. One can change the relative weighting of cost within the BCA criteria or assume the cost of an alternative will be higher or lower. These scenarios only require changing a few numbers in a spreadsheet and can quickly be provided.[55]

---

[55] BCA analysts should complete these alternate scenario calculations (sensitivity analysis) prior to the *emerging results* presentation. Then, when asked questions such as "What if we have underestimated the cost of alternative # 4 by $2M?" the answer as to how this would affect the overall scoring between alternatives can immediately be provided. This is especially helpful in enabling the decision maker(s) to isolate what issues warrant further attention.

Appendix D: Other Reference Sources

1. Guidebook for Performance-Based Services Acquisition (PBSA) in the Department of Defense, December 2000.
2. Guiding Principles for Performance-Based Logistics (PBL) Implementation Within the U.S. Army Materiel Command (AMC), 29 September 2006.
3. U.S. Army Performance-Based Logistics (PBL) Business Case Analysis (BCA) Policy, 18 August 2005
4. Department of the Navy Guide for Developing Performance Based Logistics Business Case Analyses (P07-006), November 06, 2007
5. Schmidt, Marty. The Business Case Guide. 2nd ed. Solution Matrix Ltd: May 2002.
6. Department of the Army Cost Analysis Manual, U.S. Army Cost and Economic Analysis Center, May 2002

Appendix E: Acronyms

AMC	Army Materiel Command
APB	Approved Program Baseline
BCA	Business Case Analysis
DoD	Department of Defense
ERP	Enterprise Resource Planning
EVMS	Earned Value Management System
IPT	Integrated Product Team
IRR	Internal Rate of Return
LCCE	Life Cycle Cost Estimate
NPV	Net Present Value
OMB	Office of Management & Budget
OSD	Office of the Secretary of Defense
PBL	Performance Based Logistics
ROI	Return on Investment
SCM	Supply Chain Management
SME	Subject Matter Expert

ISBN 1-933912-23-5

First Edition, January 2008

Westview Publishing Co., Inc.
P.O. Box 210183
Nashville, TN 37221
www.westviewpublishing.com

Printed in the United States
104505LV00001B